Prosperous Parenting

Steps to Building Your Child's Financial Future

Benjamin Sterling

Copyright © 2023 by Benjamin Sterling

All rights reserved.

No portion of this book may be reproduced in any form without written permission from the publisher or author, except as permitted by U.S. copyright law.

Contents

1. Introduction — 1
2. Money Basics — 6
3. Introduction to Investing — 26
4. Building a Strong Financial Foundation — 35
5. Money Management Skills — 42
6. The Role of Money in Life — 63
7. Preparing for Big Moments — 93
8. Learning about Financial Changes — 112
9. Conclusion — 123

Chapter One

Introduction

As a parent, you're the primary influence on your child's financial habits and attitudes. This book is designed to be your companion as you navigate the rewarding task of introducing your child to the world of money management. Whether you have a toddler who's just learning to count or a pre-teen starting to ask more complex questions about money, you'll find valuable insights and tips here.

Before diving into teaching your child, it's essential to assess your own financial knowledge. Don't worry if you're not a finance expert; the key is to be open to learning along with your child. This process is not just about teaching—it's also about growing and reinforcing your financial understanding. Throughout this book, we'll revisit some basic financial concepts and introduce ways to discuss them with your child.

Your attitude towards money will significantly influence how your child perceives financial matters. It's important to approach financial education with a positive and proactive mindset. Emphasize the opportunities that come with good money management, such as security, freedom, and the ability to help others, rather than focusing solely on the limitations of budgeting or saving.

One of the most effective ways to teach children about money is through everyday experiences. Shopping trips, saving for a toy, or even playing games can be excellent opportunities for learning. In this book, we'll explore how to use these everyday moments to introduce basic financial concepts in a way that is engaging and age-appropriate.

Involve your child in setting simple financial goals. This could be as straightforward as saving for a small toy or planning a family outing. Goal setting helps children understand the value of money and the satisfaction of achieving a target through patience and perseverance. We'll discuss techniques to make goal setting a fun and educational experience.

Every child is unique, and so is their understanding and interest in money. You'll learn how to tailor your financial discussions to suit your child's age, maturity level, and interests. This personalized approach ensures that your child remains engaged and absorbs the most from these lessons.

Both you and your child will make mistakes along the way, and that's okay! Financial missteps are invaluable learning opportunities. This book will guide you on how to turn these mistakes into teachable moments without any guilt or stress.

The Importance of Financial Education for Kids

In today's world, where financial decisions have become more complex than ever, teaching children about money is not just a luxury—it's a necessity. Financial education is as crucial as academic education, yet it often doesn't receive the same emphasis. By introducing children to financial concepts early, we empower them to navigate the world with confidence and competence.

The benefits of financial education for kids are far-reaching. It's not just about learning to save or budget; it's about developing a holistic understanding of money and its role in our lives. Children who learn about finances early are better equipped to avoid debt, save for their future, and make informed financial decisions. This knowledge lays the foundation for long-term financial stability and success.

But financial education is not just about the mechanics of money management. It's also about instilling values such as responsibility, delayed gratification, and the importance of planning. When children learn to manage money, they are also learning about setting priorities, making choices, and understanding the consequences of their decisions. These are life skills that extend far beyond the realm of finance.

Moreover, in a world increasingly driven by consumerism, financial education helps children become critical thinkers. It teaches them to question and understand the difference between wants and needs, helping them navigate a world full of advertising and marketing messages that encourage spending.

Additionally, financial literacy fosters a sense of independence and self-efficacy. Children who understand money are more likely to develop confidence in their ability to control their financial future. This sense of empowerment is pivotal as they grow into adults who can handle life's financial challenges with poise and knowledge.

Finally, by teaching your children about money, you are also setting an example. You demonstrate the importance of being informed and proactive about financial matters.

This not only benefits your children but also contributes to the creation of a financially literate and responsible society.

The importance of financial education for kids cannot be overstated. It is a gift that will continue to benefit them throughout their lives, equipping them with the knowledge, skills, and values necessary to make wise financial decisions. As we delve into the specifics of how to impart this education effectively, remember that your role as a parent is pivotal in shaping your child's financial future.

Simplifying Complex Financial Concepts

One of the biggest challenges in teaching children about finance is breaking down complex concepts into understandable and relatable ideas. This book is designed to guide you through this process, ensuring that financial learning is both accessible and engaging for your child.

Firstly, the key to simplifying financial concepts is to start with the basics and build upon them gradually. This involves introducing fundamental ideas like earning, saving, and spending in a straightforward manner. For instance, use everyday activities, such as grocery shopping or saving for a small toy, to illustrate these concepts. By contextualizing financial terms in familiar scenarios, children can grasp their meanings more naturally.

Another effective strategy is to use storytelling and analogies. Children relate well to stories and visual imagery. Explaining a financial concept through a story that involves characters and situations they can empathize with makes the learning process much more enjoyable and memorable. For instance, you can use a story about a character saving for a special item to explain the concept of savings and patience.

Games and interactive activities are also invaluable tools. Many basic financial principles can be taught through play. Board games that involve earning money, making spending choices, or saving for goals can help children understand and apply financial concepts in a playful and low-pressure environment.

Moreover, it's important to use age-appropriate language and examples. What works for a preschooler won't necessarily resonate with a pre-teen. For younger children, focus on the very basics and use simple, concrete examples. As they grow older, you can introduce more abstract concepts and larger financial ideas.

Visual aids such as charts, graphs, and simple budget sheets can also be helpful, especially for visual learners. These tools can make abstract concepts like budgeting or saving progress more tangible. For instance, a savings chart for a desired toy can visually demonstrate the concept of growth over time and the value of patience and consistency.

In addition to simplifying concepts, it's crucial to foster an environment where questions are encouraged. Children are naturally curious, and their questions can provide insights into their understanding and help you tailor the information to their level.

Finally, remember that repetition is key. Revisiting concepts in various contexts helps reinforce the learning. It's not about a one-time lesson but an ongoing conversation about money and its role in our daily lives.

In summary, simplifying complex financial concepts for children involves starting with the basics, using relatable examples and stories, engaging in interactive activities, utilizing visual aids, encouraging questions, and repeating key ideas. This approach not only makes learning about finance fun and accessible but also lays the groundwork for a lifetime of financial literacy.

What to expect in this book

In this book, you can expect a comprehensive guide that walks you through the essential aspects of financial education for children. It's designed to be your roadmap, providing clear and actionable steps to teach your child about money in a way that's both engaging and age-appropriate.

The journey begins with laying the groundwork for financial literacy. We'll explore how to introduce basic financial concepts to children, tailored to their developmental stage. From understanding the value of money to learning about earning, saving, and spending, these initial chapters set the foundation.

As we progress, the book delves into more nuanced topics such as budgeting, smart spending, and the basics of investing. These sections are crafted to make potentially complex subjects accessible and interesting for young minds. We'll use real-life scenarios, simple exercises, and interactive activities to bring these concepts to life.

An important aspect we cover is the emotional and psychological side of money. It's crucial for children to develop a healthy attitude towards finances, understanding not just the how, but also the why of money management. This includes discussions about financial responsibility, the impact of consumerism, and the importance of giving and sharing.

Practicality is a key focus of this book. You'll find each chapter equipped with tips, tools, and techniques that you can apply in everyday life. Whether it's setting up a simple savings plan, making a family budget, or finding creative ways to earn and save money, the book offers a wealth of practical ideas that you can implement immediately.

We also address common challenges and questions that parents face in teaching their children about money. From handling allowances to dealing with the influence of peers and media on children's financial perceptions, the book provides guidance and solutions to help you navigate these issues effectively.

In addition to practical advice, the book includes stories and insights from other parents and financial experts. These real-life examples and experiences add depth and offer different perspectives on how to successfully teach children about money.

Lastly, this section is not just a guide; it's an interactive experience. At the end of each chapter, you'll find summaries, key takeaways, and reflective questions to help you consolidate your learning. There are also activities and projects that you and your child can undertake together, making financial education a collaborative and enjoyable journey.

In essence, what you can expect in this book is a promise of a comprehensive, practical, and engaging guide to financial parenting. It's a resource that grows with your child, offering valuable insights and tools at every stage of their development, helping you lay a strong foundation for their financial future.

Chapter Two

Money Basics

What is Money and Why it Matters

Money, in its essence, is a fascinating and multifaceted tool that significantly shapes our daily lives and the world at large. At its core, money is a medium of exchange, a function that has revolutionized the way we conduct transactions. Gone are the days of bartering goods directly for other goods. Instead, money provides a convenient and standardized way to value and exchange a vast array of goods and services. This simplification of trade has been a cornerstone in the development of complex economies and global markets.

But money is more than just a tool for exchange; it serves as a store of value. This aspect of money allows people to save and accumulate wealth, enabling them to plan for the future, whether it be for education, retirement, or other significant expenses. The ability to store value over time gives individuals a sense of security and control over their financial futures.

Additionally, money functions as a unit of account. It provides a standard measure for pricing goods and services, simplifying the process of comparing costs and making informed purchasing decisions. This standardization is crucial in a functioning economy, as it offers a consistent way to assess the value of goods and services.

Understanding why money matters is just as important as knowing what it is. Money is integral to our daily lives, facilitating basic transactions like buying food and paying for housing, as well as enabling us to enjoy leisure and luxury. Beyond individual use, money's role extends to a broader societal context. It's a driving force behind economic growth, influences government policies, and impacts global markets. Money is deeply intertwined with social and economic structures, affecting everything from individual choices to the fate of nations.

Teaching children about the importance of money is therefore not just about enabling them to make purchases but also about helping them understand their place in a larger economic system. It fosters an awareness of the value and power of money in shaping personal and communal futures. Children who understand the fundamental aspects of money – as a medium of exchange, a store of value, and a unit of account – are better equipped to navigate the world with confidence and make informed financial decisions.

In summary, money is a key concept that underpins much of our daily interactions and long-term planning. Its role as a medium of exchange, a store of value, and a unit of account makes it a vital component of modern society. Understanding these aspects of money helps children grasp its significance and prepares them for a future where they can manage their finances with knowledge and responsibility.

Simple Ways to Explain Money to Kids

When it comes to teaching children about money, the key is to keep it simple, relatable, and engaging. As young parents, you have numerous opportunities every day to introduce your child to the world of finance in a way that resonates with their curiosity and level of understanding.

Start by utilizing everyday experiences as teaching moments. For instance, a trip to the grocery store can become an impromptu lesson in financial transactions. Here, you can discuss why certain items cost more than others, the concept of budgeting, or the process of paying and receiving change. These real-life examples help demystify abstract financial concepts, making them more tangible for young minds.

Incorporating play into financial education is another effective strategy. Children love games, and games involving money can be both fun and educational. Playing 'store' or using board games that feature currency allows kids to handle play money, simulate transactions, and learn basic arithmetic in a playful context. This kind of hands-on experience is invaluable in helping them understand how money works in a practical setting.

Stories and visual aids are also powerful tools. Children are often captivated by stories, so using books that include lessons about money is a great way to engage their imagination and teach important financial concepts. Additionally, visual aids like piggy banks or clear jars for saving coins can visibly demonstrate the concept of saving and the joy of watching savings grow over time.

Getting children involved in financial decisions can be remarkably instructive. Allowing them to make small choices with their allowance or involving them in a family saving goal helps them understand the value and power of money. It also teaches them about decision-making and prioritizing, skills that are essential for sound financial management.

When explaining more complex concepts such as banks or credit, try to use simple analogies. For example, you could compare a bank to a giant piggy bank where people keep their money safe, or explain credit cards as a means of promising to pay the store later, like an IOU.

Encourage curiosity by welcoming questions about money. Kids often have a natural interest in new concepts, and their questions can lead to deeper discussions and understanding. Answering these questions in clear, age-appropriate language helps solidify their grasp of financial principles.

Lastly, it's important to frame conversations about money positively. Instead of solely focusing on financial limitations, emphasize the benefits of saving, planning, and thoughtful spending. This helps to foster a healthy, proactive attitude towards money.

By adopting these simple, engaging methods, you can make the process of teaching your children about money a natural and enjoyable part of everyday life. This not only helps them understand the basics of finance but also lays the groundwork for responsible and informed financial habits as they grow older.

Fun Activities to Teach Money Basics

Teaching kids about money doesn't have to be a dry, academic exercise. By incorporating fun activities into the learning process, you can engage your children's interest and make financial concepts more relatable and memorable. Here are some engaging and educational activities that can help young parents introduce their children to the basics of money:

1. **Play Store**: Set up a mock store at home with items from around the house. Label each item with a price tag. Give your child play money to 'buy' these items. This game teaches them about transactional exchanges, pricing, and the value of different items. You can also introduce the concept of change, helping them understand basic addition and subtraction.

2. **Money Jars**: Create separate jars for saving, spending, and sharing. Each time your child receives money, whether from chores or as a gift, encourage them to divide it among these jars. This activity teaches them the fundamental principles of budgeting and the importance of balanced financial planning.

3. **Family Budget Planning**: Involve your children in simple budget planning for a family event like a picnic or movie night. Show them how you allocate funds for different needs and wants. This not only teaches them about budgeting but also about making choices and trade-offs.

4. **Coin Identification and Sorting**: For younger children, learning to identify and sort different coins can be both fun and educational. You can turn this into a game, where they sort coins into different jars or sections of a piggy bank, and reward them for getting it right. This helps with their math skills and coin recognition.

5. **Pretend Restaurant**: Play a restaurant game where your child is either the customer, waiter, or chef. Use play money for transactions. This can be a fun way to teach them about the cost of items, making change, and the value of good service.

6. **Financial Board Games**: There are many board games that incorporate money management and can be great learning tools. Games like Monopoly or The Game of Life can teach children about earning, saving, and spending money, as well as the consequences of financial decisions.

7. **Goal Setting and Saving for a Toy**: Help your child set a goal to save for a toy they want. Create a chart to track their progress and show them how each contribution to their savings gets them closer to their goal. This teaches patience, goal-setting, and the satisfaction of earning something they really want.

8. **Charity and Giving**: Encourage your child to choose a charity or cause to donate a portion of their savings. Discuss with them why giving is important and how it can make a difference. This helps instill values of generosity and empathy.

By incorporating these fun activities into your child's life, you're not just teaching them about money; you're also helping them develop critical life skills like math proficiency, decision-making, and social responsibility. These activities can make learning about money an enjoyable and rewarding experience for both you and your child.

1.2 Saving Made Simple
How to Start Saving and Why It's Important

Teaching children the importance of saving and how to start is a vital step in their financial education. Saving money is not just about putting aside a portion of what one earns; it's about building a foundation for financial security and understanding the value of delayed gratification.

Why Saving is Important

Saving plays a critical role in financial well-being, both in the short and long term. Here are some key reasons why saving is important:

- **Emergency Cushion**: Saving provides a safety net for unexpected expenses, such as medical emergencies or home repairs. Teaching children to save for unforeseen circumstances can help them understand the value of being prepared.

- **Future Goals**: Savings can help achieve future goals, like buying a car, funding education, or going on a dream vacation. When children save towards a specific goal, they learn the importance of planning and working towards something they value.

- **Financial Independence**: Consistent saving habits lead to financial independence. By learning to save, children understand that they have control over their financial future. It instills a sense of responsibility and empowerment.

- **Understanding Value and Prioritization**: Saving teaches children about prioritizing needs and wants. It helps them discern the value of items and experiences, encouraging thoughtful spending.

How to Start Saving

Starting to save can be made simple and fun for children. Here's how young parents can initiate this process:

- **Regular Saving Habits**: Begin by encouraging your child to save a small, manageable portion of their allowance or any money they receive. It could be as simple as putting a few coins into a savings jar each week.

- **Visible Savings**: Use a clear jar or a piggy bank for younger children. This allows them to see their savings grow over time, which can be incredibly motivating.

- **Goal-Setting**: Help your child set a tangible saving goal. It could be a toy they've been wanting or a fun activity. Having a clear goal makes the act of saving more purposeful and rewarding.

- **Rewards for Saving**: Consider creating a matching program, where you contribute a small amount to their savings when they reach certain milestones. This not only encourages saving but also demonstrates the concept of interest or growth over time.

- **Education Through Conversation**: Regularly discuss the importance of saving with your child. Use everyday situations to highlight how saving money can be beneficial, such as pointing out items they have been able to purchase because of their savings.

- **Lead by Example**: Children learn a lot by observing. When they see their parents saving and discussing financial plans, they understand the importance of these habits.

Starting the habit of saving early instills a sense of financial discipline and awareness in children. It's not just about accumulating money; it's about understanding the value of money, planning for the future, and learning to make informed financial choices.

Easy Saving Methods for Kids

Introducing children to saving methods that are both easy and engaging can help cultivate lifelong financial habits. Here are some straightforward and effective ways to teach kids about saving:

1. **Piggy Banks and Jars**: Start with the classic piggy bank or a clear jar. A clear jar is especially effective as it allows children to see their money growing. Encourage your child to add to their piggy bank or jar regularly, whether it's with part of their allowance, money received as gifts, or coins found around the house.

2. **Chart and Sticker System**: Create a savings chart and use stickers as a fun way to track progress. Each time your child adds money to their savings, they can add a sticker to the chart. This visual representation can be very motivating, especially when they see how close they are getting to their saving goal.

3. **Matching Contributions**: Implement a matching system where you, as a parent, match a portion of your child's savings. This not only encourages them to save more but also teaches them about the benefits of employer matching in savings accounts like 401(k)s.

4. **Savings Goals**: Help your child set realistic and achievable savings goals.

Whether it's a toy, a book, or a special outing, having a tangible goal can make saving more meaningful and rewarding. Discuss with them how long it might take to reach their goal and what amount they need to save regularly.

5. **Earned Allowances**: Instead of automatically giving allowances, tie them to chores or tasks. This method helps children understand that money is earned. It can also be an opportunity to discuss saving a portion of their earnings.

6. **Use of Technology**: There are many apps and online tools designed to teach children about saving and managing money. These digital platforms can be particularly appealing to older children and can provide a more interactive and modern approach to saving.

7. **Regular Savings Reviews**: Have regular discussions about their savings progress. This could be a monthly sit-down where you count their savings together and talk about what they're saving for. It's a great way to show them how small amounts can add up over time.

8. **Gift Contributions to Savings**: Encourage family members to consider contributing to your child's savings in lieu of traditional gifts for birthdays or holidays. This can help boost their savings and teach them about long-term gratification.

9. **Visual Savings Goals**: For visual learners, use a poster or a board to depict what they are saving for. For instance, if they're saving for a bicycle, have a picture of the bike and a progress bar they can fill in as they save.

10. **Savings Account for Older Kids**: For older children, opening a savings account in their name can be a great educational experience. It introduces them to how banks operate and the concept of earning interest on savings.

By incorporating these methods, you can make saving an enjoyable and integral part of your child's routine. These strategies not only teach kids how to save but also about the value of money and financial planning.

Setting up a Piggy Bank or a Simple Savings Account

Introducing children to the concept of saving through tangible means like a piggy bank or a savings account is a crucial step in their financial education. Here's how you can go about it:

Setting Up a Piggy Bank

1. **Choosing the Piggy Bank**: Let your child pick out their piggy bank. This could be an actual piggy bank or any money-saving container, like a clear jar. The key is to make it something they are excited about using.

2. **Location**: Place the piggy bank in a spot where your child can easily access and see it. This constant visibility serves as a reminder and encouragement to save.

3. **Initial Deposit**: Start with an initial deposit, perhaps from their allowance, a gift, or money earned from chores. Explain that this money is the beginning of their savings.

4. **Regular Contributions**: Encourage regular contributions to the piggy bank. It could be a small amount from their weekly allowance or loose change found around the house.

5. **Track Progress**: Occasionally, count the savings with your child. This can be an exciting activity, as they see their money grow. Use this opportunity to discuss what they might want to save for.

6. **Discussion on Spending vs. Saving**: Use the piggy bank as a tool to teach the difference between immediate gratification (spending right away) and delayed gratification (saving for something bigger).

Setting Up a Simple Savings Account

1. **Selecting a Bank**: Choose a bank that offers child-friendly savings accounts. Look for accounts with no fees, easy access, and perhaps an interest rate that can help teach them about how savings can grow over time.

2. **Involving Your Child**: Make the process of opening the account a learning experience. Take them to the bank with you and let them participate in the conversation.

3. **Understanding the Account**: Explain how a savings account works. Discuss

how the money they deposit in the bank will be kept safe and how it can earn interest over time.

4. **Regular Deposits**: Set up a routine for depositing money into the account. This could be a portion of their allowance, gift money, or other earnings. Many banks allow you to set up automatic transfers, which can be a useful tool for consistent saving.

5. **Monitoring the Account**: Regularly check the account balance with your child. Many banks offer online access, which can be an engaging way for your child to see their savings grow.

6. **Goal Setting**: Encourage setting savings goals. Whether it's a larger purchase or simply reaching a certain amount, having a goal can provide motivation and a sense of achievement once it's reached.

7. **Financial Literacy Discussions**: Use this as an opportunity to have broader discussions about financial responsibility, the importance of saving, and how to manage money wisely.

By setting up a piggy bank and a savings account, children can learn about the basics of saving in both a tangible and more abstract way. These tools not only help them understand the concept of saving but also instill valuable financial habits that can last a lifetime.

1.3 Smart Spending

Smart spending is an essential component of financial literacy. Teaching kids how to spend money wisely involves differentiating between needs and wants, making shopping an educational experience, and understanding the concept of budgeting. Let's explore these areas:

Teaching Kids the Difference Between Needs and Wants

Helping children understand the distinction between needs and wants is a crucial step in developing their financial literacy. This concept lays the foundation for making wise spending decisions and managing money effectively. Here's how to approach this lesson:

1. **Definitions and Examples**: Start by defining 'needs' as essentials necessary for living and 'wants' as things that are nice to have but not necessary for survival. For example, food, water, and a home are needs, while toys, gadgets, and luxury

items are wants. Use everyday examples to make these definitions clear and relatable.

2. **Interactive Activities**: Engage children in activities that help them categorize different items into needs and wants. You can use pictures from magazines, draw items, or even use real objects around the house. This activity not only makes learning fun but also encourages them to think critically about each item's necessity.

3. **Storytelling and Role-Playing**: Use stories or role-playing games to illustrate scenarios where characters must choose between needs and wants. This can help children understand the consequences of these choices in a practical and engaging way.

4. **Visual Aids**: Create a chart or use a whiteboard to list items under 'needs' and 'wants'. Visual representation helps solidify the concept. You can revisit and update this chart regularly as part of an ongoing learning process.

5. **Real-Life Application**: Involve children in decision-making during shopping trips. For instance, ask them to identify if items in the cart are needs or wants. This not only reinforces the concept but also helps them apply it in real-life situations.

6. **Discuss Budgeting**: Explain how family budgets work and how they are designed to cover needs first, with wants being secondary. This can be tied into discussions about saving and prioritizing spending.

7. **Use Media and Advertisements**: Media and advertisements often blur the lines between needs and wants. Use examples from commercials or ads to discuss how marketing tries to influence consumer behavior and how to be discerning about these messages.

8. **Reflecting on Personal Choices**: Encourage children to reflect on their own choices by asking them about recent purchases or desires. Discuss if those were needs or wants and explore the reasoning behind their choices.

9. **Encouraging Empathy and Gratitude**: Discussing needs and wants can also

be an opportunity to cultivate empathy and gratitude. Talk about how different people may have different needs, and how being able to fulfill even some wants is a privilege.

By teaching the difference between needs and wants in these various ways, children learn to think more critically about their spending. It encourages a more mindful approach to money and helps them understand the importance of financial priorities and responsible decision-making.

Fun shopping trips with a learning twist

Transforming a regular shopping trip into a fun and educational experience is a wonderful way to teach children about smart spending and the value of money. When you set a budget for your outing, involve your child in the decision-making process. This can be an adventure in itself. For instance, if the budget is for groceries or new clothes, allowing them to choose items within that budget helps them understand the importance of prioritizing and making thoughtful decisions.

The grocery store is a fantastic classroom. Here, children can learn the art of price comparison. Encourage them to look at different brands or sizes of the same product and decide which offers the best value. This is not just about finding the cheapest item but understanding what 'value for money' means. It's a practical skill that will serve them well throughout life.

Coupons and discounts can turn a shopping trip into a treasure hunt. Before heading out, spend some time with your child looking for coupons online or in flyers. Use these coupons during your trip to show how much can be saved. This activity not only makes shopping more exciting but also teaches the importance of seeking out savings.

A grocery list is a roadmap for efficient shopping. Involve your child in creating this list. Discuss why each item is needed, which are essentials (needs), and which are extras (wants). This can be a practical way to understand budgeting and planning.

There's something tangibly educational about using cash for purchases. It can make the concept of spending more real for a child compared to using a credit or debit card. Handing over cash and receiving change helps them visualize and understand how money is spent and how quickly it can be used up.

While walking through the aisles, play a game of 'needs vs. wants.' This can be an enjoyable way to reinforce the concept of essential spending versus discretionary spending. It's a lesson that ties in with the bigger picture of budgeting and managing finances.

Discussing the quality of items and their pricing is another insightful aspect of shopping. Teach your child that sometimes, a more expensive item of higher quality can be more economical in the long run, compared to a cheaper but lower-quality alternative. This conversation can lead to an understanding of long-term value.

Finally, if there's an opportunity to donate, like a charity box at the checkout, involve your child. It's a chance to discuss the importance of community support and generosity. Even a small contribution can be a significant lesson in empathy and social responsibility.

In these ways, a simple shopping trip can become an enjoyable and informative journey, teaching children valuable lessons about money, budgeting, and making informed decisions. It's about turning everyday experiences into practical life lessons that children will carry with them as they grow.

Creating a Simple Family Budget

Creating a family budget is a crucial exercise in financial planning and an excellent way to involve children in understanding money management. Here's a step-by-step guide tailored for young parents looking to teach their children the basics of budgeting in a simple and engaging way:

1. **Gather Financial Information**: Start by gathering all your financial information, including income sources (like salaries or any other earnings) and expenses (such as rent/mortgage, utilities, groceries, transportation, and entertainment). This will give you a clear picture of your financial situation.

2. **Involve the Whole Family**: Make budgeting a family activity. Sit down with your children and explain what a budget is and why it's important. Use language that is age-appropriate and easy for them to understand.

3. **List Income and Expenses**: On a large sheet of paper or a digital spreadsheet, list all sources of income on one side. On the other side, list all monthly expenses. Be as comprehensive as possible. This visual can help children grasp the concept of money coming in and going out.

4. **Categorize Expenses**: Break down expenses into categories like 'Needs' (rent, food, utilities), 'Savings' (emergency fund, education), and 'Wants' (entertainment, dining out). This categorization helps children understand the difference between essential and non-essential spending.

5. **Set Savings Goals**: Include savings as a crucial part of your budget. Discuss with

your children the importance of saving for future goals, emergencies, or large purchases. This teaches them the value of saving and planning for the future.

6. **Allocate Money to Each Category**: Decide how much money goes into each category. Ensure that your total expenses do not exceed your income. Involve your children in this process to give them a sense of participation and decision-making.

7. **Use Visual Tools**: Consider using jars, envelopes, or a whiteboard to visually represent different budget categories. This can be particularly helpful for younger children to understand how money is allocated.

8. **Track and Review Regularly**: Keep track of your spending throughout the month. Sit down with your family regularly to review the budget and discuss how well you are sticking to it. This is a great opportunity to celebrate successes or identify areas for improvement.

9. **Adjust as Needed**: Life is unpredictable, and your budget should be flexible. If you find that you're consistently overspending in one category, it might be time to adjust your budget. Involve your children in these discussions to teach them about adapting to changing circumstances.

10. **Reinforce the Learning**: Use real-life situations to reinforce what the budget means. For example, if there's a request for a non-essential item, refer back to the budget and discuss whether it fits within the 'wants' category.

By following these steps, you can create a simple family budget that not only keeps your finances on track but also serves as a valuable teaching tool for your children. It's an engaging way to introduce them to the concepts of income, expenditure, saving, and responsible financial management.

1.4 The Joy of Earning

Teaching children about earning money is as important as teaching them how to save and spend it. This section of the book will explore how young parents can introduce their children to the concept of earning, emphasizing the value of hard work and creativity.

Simple Ways Kids Can Earn Money

Empowering children to earn money through age-appropriate activities not only teaches them valuable life skills but also fosters a sense of responsibility and independence. Here are some additional ideas for simple ways kids can earn money:

1. **Yard Work**: Depending on their age and physical capabilities, children can take on yard work tasks like raking leaves, weeding, watering plants, or planting flowers for neighbors or family members.

2. **Pet Sitting or Dog Walking**: If your child loves animals, offer pet sitting or dog walking services to neighbors or friends who have pets. This not only earns them money but also builds trust in their responsibility.

3. **Lemonade Stand**: Hosting a lemonade stand is a classic way for kids to earn money during warm weather. They can learn about sales, customer service, and basic math skills while having fun.

4. **Babysitting**: For older children with responsible and mature qualities, babysitting for younger siblings or neighbors can be a rewarding way to earn money. Ensure they have basic knowledge of child safety and first aid.

5. **Tutoring**: If your child excels in a particular subject or skill, they can offer tutoring services to younger students. This not only helps them earn money but also reinforces their own understanding of the subject matter.

6. **Craft Sales**: If your child enjoys crafting or making handmade items, they can sell their creations at local craft fairs, online marketplaces, or to friends and family.

7. **Tech Help**: Tech-savvy kids can offer assistance with basic computer or smartphone tasks to older adults who may need help navigating technology.

8. **Car Washing**: Help your child set up a car washing service in your driveway. They can wash cars for family members or neighbors, and you can teach them about pricing and customer service.

9. **Gardening**: Growing vegetables, herbs, or flowers and selling them at a local farmers' market can be an enjoyable way for children to learn about gardening, entrepreneurship, and money.

10. **House Cleaning**: Older children can offer light house cleaning services to busy families or elderly neighbors. This teaches them responsibility and time management.

11. **Book Reading**: Younger children who love reading can offer to read books to younger siblings or family friends for a small fee. This encourages their reading skills and helps them earn money.

12. **Photography**: If your child has an interest in photography, they can take photos at family events, parties, or even for school yearbooks. They can earn money by selling their photography services.

13. **Homemade Snacks**: Encourage kids to bake cookies, cupcakes, or other homemade snacks and sell them at local events or to friends and family.

14. **Odd Jobs**: Offer to do odd jobs for neighbors, such as helping with moving furniture, organizing garages, or painting fences.

15. **Virtual Assistance**: Older children can offer virtual assistance services, such as data entry, research, or administrative tasks, to individuals or small businesses.

When introducing these earning opportunities to children, emphasize the importance of responsibility, reliability, and delivering quality work. Encourage them to save a portion of their earnings, reinforcing the value of both earning and managing money wisely.

The Value of Hard Work and Earning

Discussing and demonstrating the value of hard work is crucial in helping children appreciate the effort that goes into earning money. Key points to cover might include:

- **Earning as a Reward for Effort**: Explain how money is often a reward for hard work and dedication. This helps instill a work ethic and an understanding that effort can lead to tangible results.

- **Balancing Work and Play**: Teach children the importance of balancing earning activities with schoolwork and leisure. This lesson is vital for developing time management skills and a healthy work-life balance.

- **Pride in Earning**: Encourage children to take pride in their work and the money they earn. It's important they understand that earning their own money is an achievement and something to be proud of.

Small Business Ideas for Young Entrepreneurs

Fostering an entrepreneurial spirit in children can be both fun and educational. Here are a few small business ideas:

- **Lemonade Stand or Bake Sale**: Classic and simple, these are great ways for kids to learn about sales, marketing, and customer service.

- **Handmade Crafts**: Encourage children to create and sell items such as bracelets, artwork, or homemade greeting cards.

- **Gardening Services**: For children who enjoy outdoor activities, gardening services like weeding or planting can be a great way to earn money.

- **Online Business**: Older children can explore online opportunities, such as starting a blog, a YouTube channel, or selling products on a small scale. This introduces them to digital marketing and online commerce.

In this section, children will learn that earning money can be fulfilling and enjoyable. It's an opportunity for them to discover their interests and talents, develop new skills, and understand the real-world application of working and earning. This knowledge not only prepares them for future financial responsibilities but also contributes to their overall personal growth.

The Value of Hard Work and Earning

Teaching children the importance of hard work and earning money is a foundational step in building financial literacy. Begin by integrating simple, daily tasks that can earn them rewards, such as tidying up their room, assisting in household chores, or completing homework on time. These tasks, though small, mirror the concept of working for a reward, akin to adults working for a salary.

To deepen their understanding, have open conversations about how adults earn money. Share in simple terms how your job or daily work translates into earning money. This helps them realize that money is a result of hard work and effort.

Use everyday opportunities to instill the value of earning. For instance, when your child wishes to purchase a new toy or game, discuss how they might earn the money for it. This could be through extra chores, good behavior, or excelling in a task. It's a practical lesson in earning and the satisfaction of purchasing something with money they've worked for. Encourage them to save a portion of their earnings, teaching them the value of saving and delayed gratification.

Small Business Ideas for Young Entrepreneurs

Young minds are often brimming with creativity and energy, making them ideal candidates for simple entrepreneurial ventures. Here are a few business ideas that can nurture their entrepreneurial spirit:

1. Lawn Mowing and Yard Care: Children can offer to mow lawns and maintain yards in their neighborhood. This includes mowing grass, trimming edges, and even basic gardening. It teaches responsibility and the value of hard physical work.

2. Pet Sitting/Dog Walking: For animal lovers, pet sitting or dog walking is perfect. Kids can look after pets while neighbors are away or walk dogs in the afternoons. It teaches compassion, responsibility, and time management.

3. Babysitting: Older children can offer babysitting services to families in the community. It's a great way to learn about caring for others, basic first aid, and managing small crises.

4. Car Washing: Setting up a car wash station in the driveway can attract neighbors and friends. This teaches about service quality, pricing, and marketing.

5. Bake Sale: Children can bake cookies, cakes, or other treats and sell them. This helps them learn about following recipes, the concept of cost vs. price, and customer service.

6. Craft Making and Selling: Creating crafts like bracelets, pottery, or homemade cards and selling them teaches about creativity, production costs, and the basics of commerce.

7. Tutoring Services: If a child excels in a subject like math or a language, they can tutor younger kids. This reinforces their knowledge and teaches them how to communicate and teach effectively.

8. Lemonade Stand: A lemonade stand teaches the basics of business - investment (buying ingredients), production (making lemonade), and sales (selling the drink).

9. Gardening Service: Offering to plant, weed, or water gardens for neighbors can be both educational and profitable, teaching about botany and business simultaneously.

10. Homework Help Service: Assisting peers or younger students with homework or projects can develop communication skills and reinforce their own learning.

11. Custom T-Shirt Designing: Using simple online tools to design custom t-shirts and sell them can introduce children to digital tools and online marketing.

12. Book Club/Organizer: Starting a book club for peers teaches organizational skills, communication, and can encourage a love for reading.

13. Plant Sale: Growing and selling plants or flowers, either from home or at a local market, teaches about botany, business, and patience.

14. Recycling Service: Collecting recyclable materials from neighbors can teach environmental stewardship and organizational skills.

15. Computer/Technology Help: Assisting with basic tech tasks like setting up emails or teaching how to use software can be a great service for the less tech-savvy.

16. Grocery Shopping Helper: Helping those who are unable or too busy to shop themselves can be a great service, teaching responsibility and time management.

17. House Cleaning Service: Offering cleaning services like dusting, vacuuming, or window washing teaches diligence and attention to detail.

18. Online Product Sales: Selling products online under parental supervision can introduce e-commerce skills, digital marketing, and online communication.

19. Photography Services: Offering to take photos at events or for family portraits can nurture a creative skill and teach about service delivery and editing.

20. Music Lessons: Teaching a musical instrument to younger children can develop leadership and teaching skills, along with reinforcing their own musical abilities.

These ideas not only help children learn about earning money but also equip them with life skills that will be beneficial in their future endeavors. Each business idea carries lessons in responsibility, work ethics, financial management, and interpersonal skills. Through these activities, children learn valuable life skills like responsibility, time management, and the basics of running a business. They also get a practical understanding of earning and managing money.

1.5 Introduction to Giving

Teaching the Importance of Sharing and Giving

Sharing and giving are foundational values that, when taught early in life, can significantly shape a child's character and outlook. Teaching children about the importance of giving helps them develop empathy, compassion, and a sense of community. Begin by encouraging them to share toys and snacks with friends and siblings. Explain how sharing makes others happy and creates a more enjoyable and cooperative environment.

In daily life, demonstrate acts of kindness and generosity. Children learn by example, so when they see you giving to others, they are more likely to emulate that behavior. Discuss with them why you choose to give, whether it's helping a neighbor or donating to a charity.

Ways to Donate and Help Others

Introduce your child to the concept of donation, which can be more than just monetary. Encourage them to donate old toys, books, and clothes they no longer need. This teaches them about letting go of material possessions and the joy of providing for someone else's needs.

Involve them in choosing charities or causes to donate to. This could be anything from animal shelters to food banks. Explain the purpose of these organizations and how their donations, whether small or large, make a difference.

Participate in community service projects together. Activities like volunteering at a local shelter, participating in a charity walk, or helping out in a community garden are great ways for children to experience giving back to the community firsthand.

The Joy of Being Generous

Help children understand that giving is not just about the act itself but the happiness and fulfillment that comes with it. Share stories and examples of people helping each other and the positive outcomes of these actions.

Celebrate their acts of generosity, no matter how small. Praise them when they share or donate, reinforcing that their actions are valuable and appreciated. This acknowledgment can boost their confidence and encourage continual generosity.

Encourage them to reflect on how giving makes them feel. Often, children find joy and pride in being able to help others. This reflection helps build their emotional intelligence and understanding of the impact of their actions.

By introducing the concept of giving and its importance, children learn to appreciate what they have and develop a sense of responsibility towards others. It's a vital part of building a compassionate and caring individual.

Chapter Three

Introduction to Investing

Simplified explanation of investing

Investing is a way to grow your money, similar to how a plant grows from a tiny seed. When you invest, you're essentially putting your money into something, like a savings account, stocks, or real estate, with the hope that over time, it will become more valuable. Just like a plant needs water and sunlight to grow, your investment needs time and sometimes a little risk to grow.

Imagine if you bought a small tree and planted it in your backyard. Over the years, as you take care of it, it grows bigger and stronger. In the world of money, investing works similarly. You might buy a small amount of a company's stock (which means you own a tiny part of that company). Over time, if the company does well, your small piece of the company becomes more valuable.

The key is patience and understanding that investing is for the long term. It's not about making a quick profit but about letting your money grow steadily over time. Think of it as a journey, not a sprint. It's about making smart choices now for a better, more secure future.

Why investing is important for the future

Investing is crucial for future financial security. It's like preparing for a long journey where you need to gather enough resources to last the entire trip. Just as you save food and water for a hike, investing prepares you for long-term financial needs such as retirement, your child's education, or even unforeseen emergencies.

Think of investing as a way to make your money work for you. Over time, money that is invested wisely grows, thanks to compound interest and market growth. This growth can outpace inflation, meaning the money you invest now will be worth more in the future, maintaining or increasing its purchasing power.

Moreover, investing early gives you the advantage of time. The longer your money is invested, the more opportunity it has to grow. This is often referred to as the 'time value of money'. A small amount invested today could be worth much more in the future, thanks to the power of compounding returns.

Investing is not just about building wealth, but also about financial resilience. It helps you build a cushion that can protect you and your family from life's uncertainties and ensures that you're better prepared for any financial challenges that may come your way in the future.

Stories to Illustrate Basic Investment Concepts

1. **The Tale of Two Siblings and their Savings**: This story follows two siblings, Alex and Jamie, who each receive the same weekly allowance. Alex spends his allowance right away, while Jamie decides to invest a portion of hers. Over time, Jamie's investments grow, and she can afford a much-wanted bicycle, showing the benefits of patience and long-term investing.

2. **The Gardener's Diverse Garden**: A gardener plants a variety of seeds (representing a diverse investment portfolio). Some seeds grow quickly, some take longer, and some don't grow at all. The story demonstrates the importance of diversification in investments, showing that not all investments will succeed, but a varied portfolio can still thrive overall.

3. **The Patient Fisher**: This story is about a fisher who casts a wide net and waits patiently for a big catch, symbolizing the concept of long-term investing. The fisher's patience and strategy contrast with another who quickly grabs at any small fish, representing short-term, less thought-out financial decisions.

These stories use simple, relatable scenarios to illustrate fundamental investment principles, making them accessible and understandable for readers of all ages, especially children.

2.2 Easy Investment Options
Introduction to Child-Friendly Investment Options

Introducing children to investments starts with choosing options that are straightforward and engaging. Savings accounts specifically tailored for kids are an ideal beginning. These accounts are not just places to store money; they often come with tools and resources designed to educate children about financial concepts. Through interactive features and incentives, these accounts make the process of saving and earning interest an exciting adventure for young minds.

Another child-friendly investment option is bonds. They are typically lower risk compared to stocks and provide a more stable investment route. Government savings bonds or education bonds are especially suitable for children as they are secure and have a direct connection to the child's future, such as funding their education. Bonds teach the concept of lending money and earning interest over time, offering a practical lesson in long-term financial planning.

As children grow older and their understanding of money develops, introducing them to stocks can be a beneficial step. Selecting stocks from companies that resonate with them, like their favorite toy or technology brands, can make the investment more relatable and interesting. This approach helps demystify the stock market and teaches them about ownership in a company, dividends, and the importance of market research.

To solidify these concepts, using real-life examples and stories is crucial. Narratives about how a particular investment grew over time or an individual who benefited from early investing can make these abstract ideas more tangible. These stories not only educate but also inspire and motivate children to think about their financial future in a practical and proactive manner.

How to choose the right investment

When choosing the right investment for children, it's essential to consider factors like the child's age, interests, and the intended purpose of the investment. For younger kids, simple and tangible options like savings accounts or government bonds are ideal. They offer security and an easy-to-understand growth mechanism. As children grow older, introducing them to stocks, particularly in companies they're familiar with, can be a good step. However, it's important to balance the potential for higher returns with the risks involved.

Understanding the child's goals is key. Whether it's saving for a big purchase or for future education, different objectives might call for different investment strategies. For short-term goals, choose more liquid and low-risk investments. For long-term goals, you might consider options that offer higher growth potential.

Risk tolerance is another crucial factor. Young investors typically benefit from a more conservative approach, but this can be adjusted based on the time horizon of the investment. The longer the investment period, the more potential there is to recover from market downturns, which may allow for a slightly riskier, potentially higher-return investment.

Diversification is an important concept to introduce. Explain that investing everything in one type of asset can be risky, and show how a mix of different investments can spread out that risk.

Finally, involving the child in the investment process is essential for their financial education. Discuss different options, their pros and cons, and use practical tools or games to illustrate complex concepts. The aim is to make an informed decision together while educating the child about the fundamentals of investing.

Setting up a simple investment plan

Setting up a simple investment plan for a child starts with defining clear investment goals. These can range from short-term objectives like buying a new toy to long-term goals such as saving for college. Next, determine the investment amount and frequency, which could be a portion of the child's allowance, gift money, or a fixed sum from parents. Choosing the right investment vehicle is crucial and should be based on the child's age, the goal of the investment, and the family's risk tolerance. Options might include savings accounts for younger children and bonds or stocks for older ones. It's important to regularly involve the child in monitoring the investment, using it as an educational opportunity to teach them about the nature of investments, market fluctuations, and the importance of patience and long-term planning.

To set up a simple investment plan for a child, follow these steps:

1. **Identify Goals**: Clearly define the investment goals, whether for short-term needs like a special purchase or long-term objectives like education savings.

2. **Determine Amount and Frequency**: Decide the amount to be invested and the frequency (weekly, monthly, or on special occasions like birthdays).

3. **Choose the Investment Vehicle**: Select an appropriate investment option based on the child's age, goals, and risk tolerance, such as savings accounts, bonds, or stocks.

4. **Involve the Child**: Regularly involve the child in monitoring and discussing the investment to teach them about financial growth, market dynamics, and the

value of patience and strategic planning.

2.3 The Power of Compounding
Explaining compounding in easy terms

Compounding in investing can be likened to a snowball rolling down a snow-covered hill. Imagine you start with a small snowball (your initial investment) at the top of a hill. As it rolls down, it picks up more snow (interest). The interesting part is that the snowball doesn't just grow from the original snowball's surface; it also grows from the new layers of snow it picked up along the way (this is the interest on your interest). This means as time passes, the snowball gets bigger not just because of the initial snowball but also because of all the additional snow it has gathered on its journey downhill. This illustrates how even small investments can grow significantly over time through the power of compounding.

How small investments grow over time

Small investments grow over time due to the power of compounding interest. This phenomenon can be illustrated through a simple example: Suppose a child invests $100 with an annual interest rate of 5%. In the first year, the investment grows by $5 (5% of $100), making the total $105. In the second year, the interest is calculated on the new total ($105), not just the original $100. So, the investment now grows by $5.25, making the new total $110.25. This pattern continues year after year, with the interest each year calculated on the growing amount. Over many years, even a small initial investment can grow substantially as the interest accumulates and is compounded. This demonstrates the significant impact of time and compound interest on investments, even small ones.

Fun compounding exercises for kids

Teaching kids about the power of compounding can be both fun and educational. Through interactive exercises, children can grasp how small, consistent investments grow over time, thanks to the magic of compound interest. These exercises not only introduce them to important financial concepts but also engage them in a playful and memorable way. Let's explore three creative ideas for compounding exercises that can help young minds understand and appreciate the value of saving and investing over time.

1. **Compound Interest Chart Activity**: Create a chart or graph for kids to plot the growth of an initial investment with compound interest over a period. Each week or month, they add in the new amount, seeing how the investment grows. This visual representation helps them understand how interest accumulates over time.

2. **Savings Growth Game**: Develop a simple board game where children 'invest' play money and move around a board that simulates the passing of time. Each round, they calculate the compound interest on their investment, teaching them about the growing impact of compounding.

3. **Interactive Online Calculators**: Use online compound interest calculators where children input different variables like initial amount, interest rate, and time. They can experiment with different scenarios to see how changing one factor affects the growth of their investment. This hands-on approach allows them to explore the concept in a more dynamic way.

These fun and interactive exercises demystify the concept of compounding, making it more accessible and engaging for kids. By participating in these activities, children can develop a solid understanding of how their savings can grow over time, laying the foundation for lifelong financial literacy.

2.4 Parents Investing for Kids

How parents can invest for their child's future

Parents can invest for their child's future in various ways, creating a financial foundation that can support them into adulthood. One approach is to open a savings account specifically for the child, where regular deposits can accumulate over time. For a potentially higher return, investing in the stock market through child-friendly mutual funds or ETFs can be considered.

Education savings plans like 529 plans are also popular, offering tax advantages for future educational expenses. Additionally, buying bonds or government securities provides a safer investment avenue. It's crucial for parents to consider the time horizon and the specific goals they have for their child's future, whether it's for education, a major life event, or simply to provide a financial cushion. Regular contributions, even in small amounts, can grow substantially over time due to the power of compounding interest.

Understanding custodial accounts

Custodial accounts are special types of accounts that adults can open for a minor. These accounts are managed by the adult until the child reaches a certain age, usually 18 or 21, depending on the state. There are two main types: the Uniform Gifts to Minors Act (UGMA) accounts and the Uniform Transfers to Minors Act (UTMA) accounts. UGMA accounts can include financial assets like stocks, bonds, and mutual funds, while UTMA accounts can also hold physical assets like real estate. One key aspect of custodial accounts is that any money deposited becomes the property of the child, and the funds must be used for the child's benefit. The adult custodian manages the investment choices and any withdrawals until the child comes of age. It's also important to understand the tax implications of these accounts, as the child's unearned income may be subject to taxation.

Simple steps to start investing for your child

Starting to invest for your child is an important step in securing their financial future. Here's a simple guide to begin this journey:

1. **Define Financial Goals**: Determine what you're saving for – education, a first car, a house deposit, etc.

2. **Choose the Right Investment Vehicle**: Depending on the goal, select from savings accounts, custodial accounts, or education savings plans like a 529 plan.

3. **Set up a Regular Investment Schedule**: Consistently contribute to this investment to take advantage of compounding over time.

4. **Diversify Investments**: Spread investments across different types to balance risk and potential growth.

5. **Involve Your Child**: Teach them about saving and investing to foster financial literacy.

6. **Review and Adjust**: As your child grow, periodically review and adjust the investment strategy to align with changing needs and goals.

By following these steps, you can build a robust financial foundation for your child, teaching them valuable money management skills along the way.

2.5 Risk and Rewards

Explaining financial risks in a simple way

Explaining financial risks in a simple way involves using relatable analogies. Think of investing like planting a garden. Just as different plants have different needs and risks (some might need more sun or be more prone to pests), different investments come with different levels of risk. Stocks, for example, are like plants that can grow quickly but are more sensitive to bad weather, while bonds are more like sturdy, slow-growing plants. The risk in investing is the chance that the investment might not grow as expected or might even lose value. Just like in gardening, where not all plants thrive, not all investments will always yield positive returns.

Imagine a ship setting out to sea. Just like investments, the sea journey can be smooth or rough. High-risk investments are like sailing in stormy weather – the potential for high gains (or reaching exciting, unexplored territories) is greater, but so is the chance of encountering rough seas (or losing money). On the other hand, low-risk investments are like sailing close to the shore – safer, but with less potential for big discoveries (or large gains). It's about finding the right balance between the desire for significant gains and the tolerance for potential loss. Understanding this balance is crucial in making informed investment decisions.

Balancing risk and reward

Balancing risk and reward in investing is about finding a middle ground between safety and potential gains. It involves understanding that high-reward opportunities usually come with higher risks. To achieve balance, diversify investments across different types, sectors, and risk levels. This spreads out the potential risk, ensuring that if one investment performs poorly, others might compensate. It's also important to align investments with long-term goals and risk tolerance. Regularly reviewing and adjusting the investment portfolio as circumstances change is crucial in maintaining this balance. Teaching kids this balance helps them become cautious yet savvy investors, understanding that while taking risks is part of investing, it should be done judiciously and with informed decisions.

Teaching kids to be cautious and wise investors

To cultivate cautious and wise investors from a young age, it's essential to start with the basics of financial literacy. Begin by explaining the concept of money – not just as a means of buying things but as a tool that can grow over time when used wisely. Children can be taught the difference between saving and investing early on. Saving is like planting a seed in the ground and watching it grow slowly, while investing is like choosing the right plants for the right seasons to grow a thriving garden.

One effective method to teach children about investing is through a 'virtual stock market' game. This allows them to choose companies they're interested in, like their favorite toy manufacturer or a popular technology brand, and track the performance of these stocks over time. This not only makes the concept of investing more relatable but also helps them understand market fluctuations and the patience required in investing.

Discuss the importance of research and due diligence. Just as they do their homework for school, researching a company or an investment opportunity teaches them to make informed decisions. Encourage them to ask questions like, "What does the company do?" and "Is the company doing something that will make it successful in the long run?"

Risk is an inherent part of investing, and it's crucial for children to understand this. Use real-life examples to explain the concept of risk and reward. For instance, relate investing in high-risk stocks to a challenging game that could either lead to high points or losing points. Conversely, investing in low-risk options could be likened to a safer, more consistent game, teaching them the value of balance and diversification.

Teach them about the power of compound interest, perhaps with a simple online calculator. Show them how money can grow over time and the earlier they start investing, the more they can potentially gain. This can be a great motivation for them to start saving a portion of their allowance or gift money for investing.

Finally, it's vital to instill in them the ethics of investing. This includes understanding the responsibility that comes with investing and the impact of their investment choices on the wider world. Encourage them to think about sustainable and ethical investing, emphasizing how their investment decisions can contribute to a better future.

Remember, the goal is to make them not just smart investors but also responsible and ethical ones. It's about planting the seeds of financial wisdom that will grow with them into adulthood.

Chapter Four

Building a Strong Financial Foundation

Choosing a Child-Friendly Savings Account

The journey to wise investing begins with the foundational step of saving. For children, this is best introduced through a child-friendly savings account. When selecting such an account, focus on options that are specifically designed for young savers. These accounts often come with no maintenance fees, low minimum balance requirements, and sometimes, fun incentives like small toys or deposit match programs to encourage regular saving.

It's also crucial to involve the child in the process of choosing and opening the account. This can be a great learning experience, helping them understand the basics of banking. Explain the process of how a savings account works, how money is kept safe in a bank, and the concept of earning interest on their savings.

The Basics of Interest Rates

Interest rates are a key concept in the world of finance and a great starting point for young minds. In simple terms, interest is the money the bank pays the account holder for keeping their money in the bank. For children, this can be explained as a reward for saving their money instead of spending it immediately.

Use real numbers to make this more tangible. For instance, show them how a 1% interest rate on their savings account would increase their money over a year. If they save $100, they will have $101 at the end of the year. Although the amount might seem small, emphasize the importance of gradual growth and the concept of compound interest, where they earn interest on the interest over time.

Making Regular Saving a Fun Habit

Encouraging regular saving habits in children is vital. One way to make this fun is by setting savings goals. These goals could range from small items, like a new toy or a book, to larger goals, such as saving for a special outing. Visual aids, like a savings chart or a progress thermometer that they can color in as they save, make the process engaging and rewarding.

Another method is to establish a regular 'bank day' – a specific day of the week or month where the child deposits a part of their allowance or gift money into their savings account. This not only builds discipline but also gives them something to look forward to.

Additionally, consider rewarding their savings behavior. This doesn't have to be monetary; it could be as simple as an extra hour of playtime or a special activity. The key is to associate positive experiences with the act of saving.

By starting with a savings account, children learn the crucial first steps of financial management. They understand the value of money, the benefit of saving, and the patience required for long-term rewards. These lessons are the building blocks of becoming cautious and wise investors in the future.

3.2 Education Savings Made Easy

Simple Ways to Save for Education

Saving for your child's education can seem daunting, but with the right approach, it can be both manageable and rewarding. Start by establishing a dedicated education savings account separate from other savings. This helps in tracking progress specifically towards education goals.

Automating savings can simplify the process. Set up a monthly automatic transfer from your checking account to the education savings account. Even small amounts, when saved consistently over time, can add up significantly. Encourage family members to contribute to this fund in lieu of traditional gifts on special occasions.

Involve your child in the saving process. This can include having them contribute a small portion of their allowance or money from odd jobs. This not only helps grow the savings but also instills in them a sense of responsibility and investment in their own education.

What is a 529 Plan and How It Works

A 529 plan is a tax-advantaged savings plan designed to encourage saving for future education costs. These plans are sponsored by states, state agencies, or educational institutions and are authorized by Section 529 of the Internal Revenue Code.

There are two types of 529 plans: prepaid tuition plans and education savings plans. Prepaid tuition plans let you pre-pay all or part of the costs of an in-state public college education. Education savings plans, however, allow a saver to open an investment account to save for the beneficiary's future qualified higher education expenses, which can include tuition, room and board, and other related expenses.

The beauty of a 529 plan lies in its tax benefits. Contributions grow tax-deferred, and withdrawals are tax-free when used for qualified education expenses. Some states also offer tax benefits for contributions to a 529 plan. These plans typically offer a range of investment options, and the account owner can choose one based on their investment preference and risk tolerance.

Starting Small with Education Savings

Starting small with education savings is a practical approach. It's important to remember that even modest savings can grow over time. Begin by setting achievable goals and gradually increase your savings as your financial situation allows.

Encourage your child to contribute to their education savings from a young age. This could be through saving a portion of their birthday money or earnings from small jobs. It's also a great way to teach them about the importance of saving and investing for the future.

Review and adjust your savings plan regularly. As your income grows or your expenses change, you may find opportunities to increase the amount you save. Additionally, periodically reviewing the investment options within your 529 plan ensures that your savings strategy aligns with your risk tolerance and the time horizon for your child's education needs.

Remember, the key to successful education savings is consistency and starting as early as possible. By incorporating these simple strategies, you can ease the financial burden of your child's education and ensure a solid foundation for their academic future.

3.3 Insurance: A Simple Explanation

Basic Types of Insurance and Why They're Important

Insurance is a financial tool that helps protect individuals and families from significant financial losses due to unexpected events. It works on the principle of risk-sharing, where many people pay into a pool through premiums, and those who suffer a covered loss receive payments to help compensate them.

The most common types of insurance include:

1. **Health Insurance**: Covers the cost of medical care. It's essential because medical treatment can be very expensive, and having health insurance prevents financial disaster in case of serious illness or injury.

2. **Life Insurance**: Provides financial support to your dependents if you pass away. It's crucial for parents, as it ensures that their children will have financial support for their living expenses and education.

3. **Homeowners/Renters Insurance**: Protects your home and belongings from damage or theft. This type of insurance is important because your home is likely one of your most valuable assets.

4. **Auto Insurance**: Covers damages to your vehicle and protects you financially if you're liable for someone else's injuries or damages in an accident. Given the high cost of vehicles and medical bills, this insurance is essential for anyone who drives.

5. **Disability Insurance**: Provides income if you're unable to work due to an illness or injury. This is important because it ensures that you have a source of income even when you can't work.

Simple Examples of How Insurance Helps

- **Health Insurance**: If you have a sudden illness that requires hospitalization, health insurance can cover most of the costs, preventing you from having to pay thousands of dollars out of pocket.

- **Life Insurance**: If a parent passes away, life insurance can provide funds to help cover living expenses, education costs, and other needs for their children, ensuring financial stability during a difficult time.

- **Homeowners/Renters Insurance**: If a fire damages your home and belongings, this insurance can pay for repairs and replace lost items, helping you recover without bearing the full financial burden.

- **Auto Insurance**: If you're involved in a car accident, auto insurance can cover repair costs for your vehicle and any medical expenses if you or others are injured.

- **Disability Insurance**: If you suffer an injury that leaves you unable to work, disability insurance can replace a portion of your lost income, helping you maintain your lifestyle.

Discussing Insurance in Everyday Life

Talking about insurance in everyday life helps demystify it and makes it more relatable. For example, when driving with your children, you can explain how car insurance protects you and other drivers on the road. When visiting a doctor, you can discuss how health insurance works to cover medical costs.

Use real-life scenarios to explain the importance of insurance. For instance, if a neighbor's house suffers damage from a storm, it's an opportunity to discuss how homeowners' insurance helps in such situations. If a family member becomes ill and needs medical care, talk about how health insurance supports the family financially.

Integrating discussions about insurance into daily life not only educates children about its importance but also prepares them to make informed decisions about insurance in their future. It's about teaching them to plan ahead and protect themselves and their loved ones from unexpected financial hardships.

3.4 Goal Setting for the Future

Teaching Kids to Set Financial Goals

Setting financial goals is a fundamental aspect of financial literacy. It's important to teach children not only the value of money but also how to plan for its use. Start by discussing short-term and long-term goals. Short-term goals might include saving for a new toy or a special outing, while long-term goals could be saving for college or buying a car.

To make goal-setting effective, goals should be SMART: Specific, Measurable, Achievable, Relevant, and Time-bound. For instance, instead of a vague goal like "save money," a SMART goal would be "save $100 in six months to buy a new bicycle."

Use visual tools like charts or graphs to track progress. This makes the process tangible and helps children see the impact of their savings over time. You can also use apps or websites designed for teaching kids about money management.

Simple Goal-Setting Activities

1. **Savings Jar**: Use a clear jar to save money for a specific goal. This visual repre-

sentation of money growing can be very motivating for kids.

2. **Budgeting for a Family Outing**: Involve your child in planning and budgeting for a family activity. This could involve comparing prices, determining the amount needed, and saving towards it.

3. **Creating a Vision Board**: Encourage your child to make a vision board with pictures of their goals. This could be educational, like a college fund, or recreational, like a vacation or a new gaming console.

4. **Financial Diary**: Have your child maintain a diary or a ledger where they record their savings and spending. This not only helps in tracking their progress towards their goals but also teaches them about the importance of record-keeping in financial management.

Celebrating Financial Milestones

Recognizing and celebrating milestones is crucial in keeping kids motivated. When they reach a savings goal, celebrate with something that acknowledges their effort, like a special meal or an activity of their choice.

Use these milestones as teaching moments. For instance, when they save enough to buy something they wanted, discuss how patience and discipline helped them achieve their goal. If they fall short, discuss what they could do differently next time, emphasizing that setbacks are part of the learning process.

Additionally, introduce the concept of 'matching contributions'. For example, for every dollar they save towards a particular goal, you could contribute a certain amount. This not only motivates them but also teaches them about concepts like employer matching in retirement savings.

Long-Term Goal Setting

As children grow older, introduce more complex long-term financial goals. This could include saving for college, a car, or even starting a small business. Discuss the importance of these goals and the satisfaction and independence they bring.

Encourage them to research and understand the costs involved in these long-term goals. This research can be incorporated into goal-setting activities, making them more informed and realistic.

Teaching kids about goal setting for the future is about more than just saving money. It's about instilling values such as patience, discipline, and foresight. By starting these lessons early, you're not just preparing them to be financially savvy adults; you're giving them tools for life-long success.

Chapter Five

Money Management Skills

Creating a Simple Family Budget

A family budget is a crucial tool for managing household finances effectively. It helps in tracking income, expenses, and savings, ensuring that the family lives within its means and works towards financial goals.

1. **Start with Income**: List all sources of family income, including salaries, bonuses, and any other regular earnings.

2. **Track Expenses**: Categorize your expenses into essentials (like rent, utilities, groceries) and non-essentials (like entertainment, dining out). Keep track of all expenses for a month to understand your spending patterns.

3. **Set Spending Limits**: Based on your income and expenses, set realistic spending limits for each category. Ensure you allocate a portion of your income to savings.

4. **Review and Adjust**: Regularly review the budget and adjust as needed. Life changes, such as a new job or a growing family, will require updates to your budget.

5. **Involve the Whole Family**: Make budgeting a family activity. Discuss the budget openly and involve children in decision-making, teaching them the value of money and financial planning.

Teaching Kids to Manage Their Money

Navigating the world of finances is a crucial life skill, and the earlier it's cultivated in children, the better they are prepared for the future. In this section, we delve into practical strategies for teaching kids to manage money effectively. From a structured allowance system to understanding the fine balance between spending and saving, we aim to provide parents with actionable methods to instill sound money management habits in their children. As children grow, their financial decisions become more complex. By laying a strong foundation now, we can help them make wise choices and develop a healthy relationship with money, setting the stage for financial responsibility in their adult lives. Some of the strategies to be implemented are:

1. **Allowance Strategy**: Implement a structured allowance system where children earn money through chores or responsibilities. This teaches them the value of hard work and money. Guide them to divide their allowance into three parts: spending, saving, and sharing. This not only instills a sense of financial responsibility but also compassion and charity.

2. **Budgeting Their Expenses**: Encourage children to create a simple budget for their personal expenses. This could include money for snacks, toys, or outings with friends. Teach them to track their spending and understand the difference between impulsive and thoughtful purchases.

3. **Saving for a Big Purchase**: Guide them in saving for a more expensive item they want, like a bicycle or a video game console. This teaches patience and the value of saving over time for something important.

4. **Understanding Opportunity Cost**: Introduce the concept of opportunity cost - the idea that choosing to spend money on one thing means giving up something else. Use simple examples, like spending allowance on a toy means less money for candy.

5. **Financial Decision-Making**: Involve your children in family financial decisions appropriate for their age, such as choosing between different brands at the grocery store or planning a budget-friendly family outing. This helps them understand trade-offs and prioritizing needs over wants.

Fun Budgeting Games and Activities

Budgeting doesn't have to be a dull or daunting task, especially for kids. In fact, turning budgeting into a fun and interactive learning experience can be immensely effective in teaching children the basics of money management. This section introduces a variety of engaging games and activities that parents can use to make the concept of budgeting and financial planning appealing to children. From play money exercises to interactive online games, these activities are designed to teach children about budgeting, saving, and spending in a way that's both enjoyable and educational. Through these hands-on experiences, kids can learn the value of money, the importance of saving, and the skills of budget management in a way that resonates with their young minds. Some of the fun budgeting games and activities are:

1. **Budget Planning with Play Money**: Use play money to create a mock marketplace at home where children can 'buy' items. This teaches them to manage their money and make choices within a budget.

2. **Interactive Online Games**: There are several online games and apps designed to teach children about budgeting and money management in an interactive and engaging way. These games simulate real-life financial scenarios, helping children learn about earning, saving, and spending.

3. **Family Savings Challenge**: Initiate a family savings challenge where each member contributes to a collective goal, like a family vacation. Track the progress together on a chart or graph. This not only makes saving a joint effort but also adds an element of fun competition.

4. **DIY Restaurant at Home**: Create a pretend restaurant at home. Price each item on the menu and give each family member a budget for their meal. This activity teaches kids about budgeting for dining and the value of money in a practical setting.

5. **Expense Tracking Journal**: Encourage older children to maintain a simple expense tracking journal or use a basic budgeting app. Regularly review this with them to discuss their spending decisions and offer guidance.

6. **Financial Literacy Board Games**: Invest in board games focused on financial literacy, like 'Cashflow for Kids' or 'Easy Money', which can make learning about money management, investing, and budgeting an enjoyable experience.

By enhancing these activities, children can develop a more nuanced understanding of money management from an early age. Engaging in these activities regularly will cement their understanding and practice of sound financial habits, setting them up for a successful financial future.

4.2 Understanding Credit

In today's financial landscape, credit plays a pivotal role. Understanding credit and how it works is fundamental to financial literacy. This section aims to break down the concept of credit into understandable parts for young parents and their children. We'll explore what credit is, why it's important to have good credit, and practical ways to build a positive credit history. By instilling an understanding of credit from a young age, we can prepare children for responsible financial decisions in their future.

Basic Concept of Credit and Borrowing

Credit refers to the ability to borrow money with the understanding that it will be repaid later, often with interest. It's like getting a loan for something you need now and promising to pay back over time. Credit can be in various forms, including credit cards, loans, and lines of credit.

It's essential to teach children that credit isn't 'free money'. It comes with the responsibility of timely repayment and management. Explain how borrowing more than one can afford or failing to repay can lead to financial difficulties.

Why Good Credit Matters

Good credit is crucial because it reflects your financial reliability. It is represented by a credit score, a number that tells lenders how likely you are to repay borrowed money. A good credit score can open doors to important life opportunities like buying a house, financing a car, or even getting a job in some cases.

Explain to children that good credit is built over time by consistently paying bills on time, managing debts responsibly, and making wise financial decisions. It's much like a report card or a reputation — it takes time to build and maintain.

Simple Ways to Build a Good Credit History

1. **Timely Bill Payments**: Emphasize the importance of paying bills on time. Late payments can negatively impact credit scores.

2. **Understanding Credit Reports**: Teach older children about credit reports, which are records of your credit history. Discuss how to check credit reports and ensure their accuracy.

3. **Responsible Credit Card Use**: For teens, consider getting a secured credit card or becoming an authorized user on a parent's card to start building credit. Teach them to use it for small, manageable purchases and pay it off in full each month.

4. **Credit Education Tools**: Utilize educational resources and tools designed for young people to learn about credit. Many financial institutions offer programs and games to help understand credit concepts.

5. **The Power of Budgeting**: Reinforce that sticking to a budget is key to managing credit. It helps in making sure that one doesn't spend more than they can afford to repay.

Understanding credit is an essential part of financial education. It's about more than just borrowing money; it's about building a reputation with financial institutions that can have a long-lasting impact on one's financial future. By teaching children the basics of credit, the importance of a good credit score, and how to build a healthy credit history, we are equipping them with the tools necessary for sound financial management. This knowledge will serve them well as they grow into financially responsible adults, capable of making informed decisions about credit and debt.

4.3 Entrepreneurial Skills

Encouraging Business Thinking in Kids

Fostering a business mindset in children is a key step toward developing their entrepreneurial skills. This mindset is not just about understanding and starting businesses, but also about cultivating qualities like innovation, strategic thinking, and financial intelligence. In this detailed exploration, we'll delve into effective ways to encourage business thinking in kids, including setting up the right environment, guiding them through practical experiences, and emphasizing the importance of creativity and problem-solving.

Creating the Right Environment for Business Thinking

1. **Encourage Curiosity and Inquiry**: Always answer their 'why' and 'how' questions. Encourage them to explore how things work, why businesses succeed or fail, and what makes an idea sellable. This curiosity lays the groundwork for business thinking.

2. **Discuss Business in Daily Life**: Regularly talk about businesses in day-to-day life. When you visit a store, discuss what might make it successful, the importance of customer service, or how they advertise their products.

3. **Role Modeling**: Demonstrate entrepreneurial behaviors yourself. If you make decisions in your job or run a business, talk to your kids about your experiences, challenges, and how you overcome them.

Guiding Through Practical Business Experiences
1. **Start Small Projects**: Encourage kids to start small projects or mini-businesses. This could be a lemonade stand, a garage sale, or a small craft project. The goal is to let them experience the creation and management of a simple business.

2. **Involve in Family Business**: If you have a family business, involve your children in age-appropriate activities. Let them see how the business operates, interact with customers, or help with simple tasks.

3. **Business Case Studies**: Use stories or case studies of kid entrepreneurs. Discuss what these young individuals did, what challenges they faced, and what kids can learn from these stories.

Cultivating Creativity and Problem-Solving
1. **Brainstorming Sessions**: Regularly hold family brainstorming sessions to think of new business ideas or solve problems. Teach them to think outside the box and consider various solutions.

2. **Encourage Creative Hobbies**: Often, business ideas come from personal interests or hobbies. Support your child's interests, be it in arts, technology, or any other field, as these can be fertile ground for business ideas.

3. **Teach Risk Assessment**: Encourage them to weigh the risks and benefits of their business ideas. This helps in developing critical thinking and decision-making skills.

Encouraging business thinking in kids is about nurturing a mindset that is curious, creative, and solution-oriented. By providing them with the right environment, practical experiences, and fostering their problem-solving skills, we are not just preparing them for potential business ventures, but also equipping them with essential life skills. These skills will enable them to navigate various challenges, seize opportunities, and innovate in whatever paths they choose in their lives.

Easy and fun business projects

Engaging children in easy and fun business projects is a fantastic way to introduce them to the basics of entrepreneurship. These projects should be age-appropriate, enjoyable, and educational, providing hands-on experiences in managing money, understanding value, and learning about the market. In this detailed exploration, we will delve into a variety of business projects that not only capture the imagination of young minds but also impart fundamental business lessons.

Business Projects Ideas

1. **Bake Sale or Home Café**: If your child enjoys baking or cooking, setting up a weekend bake sale or a small home café can be a great project. It teaches them about food preparation, pricing, and customer service. They can sell cookies, cupcakes, or homemade lemonade. Involve them in budgeting for ingredients and setting prices to cover costs and make a profit.

2. **Handcrafted Jewelry or Artwork Sale**: For children interested in arts and crafts, creating and selling handmade jewelry, paintings, or decorations can be both fun and educational. They can learn about material costs, time management, and the value of their creative skills.

3. **Car Wash Service**: Starting a neighborhood car wash service can teach kids about hard work and the value of a service-based business. They can learn about pricing, advertising, and delivering a service that meets customer expectations.

4. **Gardening and Plant Sale**: Children can grow plants, vegetables, or herbs and sell them in the local community. This project educates them about biology, the growing process, and the business of selling natural products.

5. **Tutoring or Teaching Services**: Older kids can offer tutoring services in subjects they excel in, or teach skills like playing a musical instrument, coding, or art. This helps them understand the value of knowledge and the process of teaching and mentoring.

6. **Recycling and Upcycling Projects**: Encouraging kids to start a recycling or upcycling project not only teaches them about sustainability but also about the business potential in 'green' initiatives. They can create upcycled crafts or organize community recycling drives.

7. **Digital Ventures**: Tech-savvy kids might enjoy setting up a basic website for

their business, creating a blog, or even developing a simple app. This introduces them to the digital side of businesses, including online marketing and digital sales.

Maximizing Learning from Business Projects

1. **Planning and Research**: Guide them through the planning and research phase. Help them understand their target market, calculate costs, and set achievable goals.

2. **Marketing and Sales**: Teach them basic marketing skills, like creating posters, using social media (if age-appropriate), or word-of-mouth promotion. Discuss how to interact with customers and the importance of customer satisfaction.

3. **Financial Literacy**: Involve them in managing the finances of their project. Teach them how to keep records of expenses and earnings, and the basics of profit and loss.

4. **Review and Reflection**: After completing the project, review the process with them. Discuss what worked, what didn't, and what they learned. This reflection is crucial for understanding the real-world application of business concepts.

Easy and fun business projects are excellent tools for teaching kids about entrepreneurship in an engaging and practical way. These projects can ignite a passion for business, teach valuable life skills, and provide a foundation for future financial literacy. By guiding children through these projects, parents can help them understand the basics of running a business, the value of hard work, and the joy of achieving their goals.

Learning from success and failure

One of the most valuable lessons in both entrepreneurship and life is learning from success and failure. Teaching children to view both outcomes as opportunities for growth and development is crucial in nurturing resilient, adaptable, and self-aware individuals. In this section, we delve into strategies and approaches to help children understand and embrace the lessons that come from their successes and setbacks in business projects and other endeavors.

Learning from Success

1. **Celebrating Achievements**: Recognize and celebrate when children achieve their goals. This reinforces positive behavior and boosts their confidence. How-

ever, it's important to focus on the effort and strategy, not just the outcome.

2. **Analyzing Success**: Help children understand why they succeeded. Was it due to thorough planning, creativity, hard work, or effective communication? Identifying these factors helps them replicate their success in future projects.

3. **Building on Success**: Encourage children to think about how they can build on their current success. Can they expand their project, diversify, or use their learnings to try something new?

4. **Teaching Humility**: While celebrating success, it's also important to teach humility. Discuss the role of teamwork, external help, or fortunate circumstances that might have contributed to their success.

Learning from Failure

1. **Normalizing Failure**: Frame failure as a normal and expected part of learning and growing. Share stories of successful people who have failed and bounced back, emphasizing that failure is not an endpoint but a stepping stone.

2. **Encouraging Emotional Resilience**: Allow children to express disappointment, but guide them towards resilience. Teach them to face setbacks with a positive attitude and the willingness to try again.

3. **Analytical Approach to Failure**: Sit down with your child and analyze the failure. What went wrong? Was it poor planning, lack of knowledge, or unforeseen circumstances? Understanding the reasons for failure is key to learning from it.

4. **Problem-Solving Skills**: Use failure as an opportunity to develop problem-solving skills. Ask questions like, "What could we do differently next time?" or "How can we turn this setback into a learning opportunity?"

5. **Persistence and Grit**: Encourage them to not give up. Discuss the importance of persistence and the ability to continue working towards a goal despite obstacles.

Integrating Lessons from Both Success and Failure

1. **Maintaining a Balanced Perspective**: Teach children to maintain a balanced

view of both successes and failures. Neither should be overly emphasized; instead, both should be seen as integral parts of the learning journey.

2. **Documenting the Journey**: Encourage them to keep a journal or a digital record of their business experiences, including what they learned from each success and failure. This documentation can be a valuable tool for reflection and growth.

3. **Encouraging Reflective Thinking**: Regularly engage in conversations that encourage reflective thinking. Ask them what they've learned, how they've grown, and what they might do differently in the future.

Learning from both success and failure is fundamental in developing entrepreneurial skills. By guiding children through the process of analyzing their successes and setbacks, we can help them build resilience, foster critical thinking, and nurture a growth mindset.

4.4 Taxes in Simple Terms

Taxes, an essential component of our financial system, can be a complex topic. However, introducing children to the concept of taxes in simple and understandable terms is crucial for their financial literacy. This section aims to demystify taxes for young minds, explaining why taxes are important and how they work in a basic sense. Additionally, we'll explore simple tax-related activities for kids to help them grasp these concepts in a practical and engaging way.

Basic understanding of taxes

Taxes are a fundamental aspect of modern society, playing a crucial role in the functioning of governments and communities. For children, understanding taxes in basic terms is an essential step towards financial literacy and civic awareness. In this expanded section, we will delve deeper into the concept of taxes, breaking it down into more digestible parts to help young minds comprehend why taxes exist and how they function in everyday life.

Explaining the Concept of Taxes

1. **What Are Taxes?**: Taxes are mandatory contributions made by individuals and businesses to the government. You can explain this to children by comparing it to how they might contribute a part of their allowance for household needs or for a group project at school.

2. **How Taxes are Collected**: Taxes are collected in various ways. Income taxes are

taken from the money people earn, sales taxes are added to the price of items they buy, and property taxes are based on the value of owned property like houses or land.

3. **Different Types of Taxes**: Introduce them to different kinds of taxes:

   - **Income Tax**: Money taken from what people earn from their jobs or businesses.

   - **Sales Tax**: Extra money paid when buying goods or services.

   - **Property Tax**: Based on property one owns, like a house or land.

   - **Excise Tax**: Specific taxes on certain goods like gasoline, alcohol, and tobacco.

The Purpose of Taxes

1. **Funding Government Services**: Explain that taxes help pay for services that the government provides. This includes public education, healthcare, infrastructure (like roads and bridges), and public safety (like police and fire services).

2. **Supporting Public Goods**: Taxes are used to fund public goods, which are things everyone can use. Examples include parks, libraries, and street lights.

3. **Social Services**: Part of the taxes goes towards social services like unemployment benefits, welfare programs, and other types of assistance for those in need.

4. **Economic Function**: Discuss how taxes help in the overall functioning of the country's economy. They are used to regulate the economy, reduce inequalities, and fund development projects.

Understanding Tax Responsibilities

1. **Paying Taxes is a Duty**: Emphasize that paying taxes is a responsibility of every citizen and is important for the welfare of the community and country.

2. **Ethical Aspect of Taxes**: Teach children that while no one enjoys paying taxes, they are essential for the common good and help in creating a fair society.

3. **Real-life Examples**: Use examples relevant to their lives. For instance, explain

how the taxes you pay help in maintaining the roads you drive on, the schools they attend, and the playgrounds where they play.

Understanding taxes in their basic form is key for children to grasp how societies function financially. By explaining the different types of taxes, their purposes, and their impact on everyday life, we can instill in young minds a sense of responsibility and awareness about their role in society. This foundational knowledge sets the stage for more advanced financial concepts and a deeper appreciation of civic duties as they grow older.

Why we pay taxes

Understanding why we pay taxes is crucial for fostering a sense of responsibility and community in children. This concept is integral to grasping how societies function and maintain various services and infrastructures. In this detailed section, we will explore the reasons behind tax payments, the benefits they bring to individuals and communities, and how they contribute to the overall functioning of a country. This understanding is vital for children to appreciate their future roles as responsible citizens.

The Role of Taxes in Society

1. **Funding Essential Services**: Taxes are the primary source of revenue for governments. They fund essential services that individuals cannot efficiently provide for themselves, such as national defense, law enforcement, and fire protection services.

2. **Supporting Public Infrastructure**: Taxes help build and maintain public infrastructure like roads, bridges, public transportation systems, and utilities. This infrastructure is essential for the functioning of society and the economy.

3. **Public Education and Healthcare**: A significant portion of tax revenue is allocated to public education and healthcare systems. These services are crucial for the welfare and development of society, ensuring that all citizens have access to education and basic healthcare.

4. **Social Welfare Programs**: Taxes fund social welfare programs such as unemployment benefits, disability insurance, and social security. These programs provide a safety net for individuals and families during times of need, reducing poverty and supporting the vulnerable.

5. **Economic Stability and Growth**: Tax revenues help stabilize the economy by

funding government spending. They also support growth by financing infrastructure projects, research and development, and other initiatives that boost economic productivity.

6. **Redistribution of Wealth**: Taxes play a role in the redistribution of wealth, helping to reduce economic inequalities. Progressive tax systems, where higher earners pay a larger percentage of their income in taxes, contribute to a more equitable society.

Teaching the Value of Taxes to Children

1. **Civic Duty and Responsibility**: Emphasize that paying taxes is part of being a responsible citizen. It's a way of contributing to the community and ensuring that everyone can enjoy public services.

2. **Real-Life Examples**: Use examples relatable to children. Explain how their school, the local park, the roads they travel on, and the library they visit are all supported by tax dollars.

3. **Community Involvement**: Discuss how taxes help fund community centers, recreational facilities, and cultural events. This can help children see the direct benefits of taxes in their daily lives.

4. **Global Perspective**: Broaden the discussion to a global level, illustrating how taxes contribute to national projects and initiatives, such as environmental conservation and scientific research.

Taxes are a vital part of any functioning society. They enable governments to provide essential services, maintain public infrastructure, support education and healthcare, and ensure economic and social welfare. Teaching children why we pay taxes is not just about explaining financial obligations but also about instilling values of citizenship, community, and shared responsibility. Understanding the role of taxes helps children appreciate the benefits they receive from living in a well-structured society and prepares them to be informed and responsible citizens in the future.

Simple tax-related activities for kids

Engaging children in simple tax-related activities is a practical and interactive way to help them understand the concept of taxes. These activities can make the abstract idea of taxes more tangible and relatable to their daily lives. In this section, we will explore various activities and games that can be used to teach children about taxes in a fun and educational manner. These activities aim to demystify taxes and show kids how they impact the community and the role they play in society.

Activity Ideas to Teach Kids About Taxes

1. **The 'Family Government' Game**: Create a mini 'family government' where kids can play different roles, such as taxpayers, government officials, or service providers. Use play money to simulate tax collection and spending on family or household needs, like groceries or utilities.

2. **Mock Store with Sales Tax**: Set up a pretend store where children can buy and sell items using play money. Add a 'sales tax' to each purchase to illustrate how taxes are added to goods in real life. Discuss how this extra money is used for public services.

3. **Lemonade Stand with Taxes**: If kids set up a lemonade stand, introduce the concept of taxes by having them set aside a small percentage of their earnings as 'tax.' Explain how in real businesses, a part of income goes to taxes.

4. **Budget Allocation Exercise**: Give kids a certain amount of play money and a list of community needs (like parks, schools, roads). Have them allocate their 'taxes' to these services, teaching them about budgeting and prioritization.

5. **Role-Playing Public Services**: Engage in role-playing where some kids act as service providers (like teachers, police officers, or librarians) paid through 'taxes' collected from others. This helps them understand how taxes fund different community roles.

6. **Income Tax Simulation**: For older children, create a simple income tax simulation. Assign them pretend jobs with salaries and demonstrate how a portion of their income would go to taxes. Use a simple percentage to calculate the tax to keep it understandable.

7. **Tax History Lesson**: Incorporate a brief history lesson about taxes in different cultures or significant historical events related to taxes (like the Boston Tea Party). This can make learning about taxes more engaging and give a broader perspective.

8. **Community Service Projects**: Link the concept of taxes to community service. Engage in a community cleanup or a charity drive and explain how such initiatives are often supported by tax-funded entities.

9. **Debate on Tax Spending**: Host a family debate on how tax money should be spent. Present different options (education, infrastructure, healthcare) and discuss the pros and cons of each, helping kids learn about the complexities of budget allocation.

Through these simple yet informative activities, children can gain a practical understanding of how taxes work and why they are important. These activities not only teach the basics of taxation but also encourage critical thinking about public spending and civic responsibility. By making tax education interactive and relevant to their everyday experiences, we can help children appreciate the role of taxes in society and their future responsibilities as taxpayers.

4.5 Digital Money

In an increasingly digital world, understanding digital transactions and online financial management is crucial. This section aims to introduce the concept of digital money to children, providing them with the knowledge and tools they need to navigate this modern financial landscape safely and wisely. We will cover the basics of digital transactions, online banking, and the importance of cybersecurity in finance. By familiarizing children with these concepts, we prepare them for a future where digital transactions are the norm, ensuring they are equipped to manage their finances securely and efficiently.

Introduction to digital transactions

In the current digital era, the concept of money and how it is used has evolved significantly. Digital transactions, an integral part of this evolution, are reshaping the way we handle financial activities. Understanding digital transactions is crucial for children growing up in this digital age. This expanded introduction aims to provide a comprehensive understanding of digital transactions, covering their various forms, how they work, their benefits, and the basic principles of using them responsibly.

Understanding Digital Transactions

1. **Definition and Explanation**: Digital transactions refer to the exchange of money through electronic means. They include any transfer of funds initiated through electronic devices like computers, smartphones, or tablets. This can range from online shopping and electronic bill payments to digital wallets and

peer-to-peer payment apps.

2. **Types of Digital Transactions**:

    - **Online Payments**: Using the internet to pay for goods and services, often through e-commerce websites or mobile apps.

    - **Electronic Fund Transfers (EFT)**: Moving money between bank accounts electronically, including online banking transfers, direct deposits, and automatic bill payments.

    - **Digital Wallets and Payment Apps**: Services like PayPal, Apple Pay, or Google Wallet, where users store money digitally to make online and in-store purchases or send money to others.

    - **Contactless Payments**: Transactions that use NFC (Near Field Communication) technology, allowing customers to tap their card or smartphone on a reader to make a payment.

    - **Cryptocurrencies**: Digital or virtual currencies, like Bitcoin, that use cryptography for secure transactions, operating independently of a central bank.

3. **How Digital Transactions Work**: Explain the process of digital transactions, from the initiation of payment (like clicking 'Pay Now' on a website) to the actual transfer of money from one account to another. Highlight the roles of different entities involved, such as banks, payment gateways, and merchant accounts.

4. **Benefits of Digital Transactions**:

    - **Convenience**: They can be conducted anytime and anywhere, eliminating the need to carry cash or visit a bank.

    - **Speed**: Transactions are often instantaneous or take considerably less time than traditional methods.

    - **Tracking and Management**: Digital records of transactions make it easier to track spending and manage finances.

- **Security**: Advanced security measures, such as encryption and fraud monitoring, help protect against theft and unauthorized access.

5. **Principles of Responsible Use**:

    - **Understanding Value**: Emphasize that digital money is real money. It's essential to understand the value of money, even when it's not physically seen.

    - **Budgeting and Control**: Teach the importance of budgeting and keeping control over spending, as digital transactions can sometimes lead to impulsive buying.

    - **Privacy and Information Security**: Stress the importance of keeping personal and financial information secure and being cautious about sharing such information online.

Introducing children to digital transactions is not just about teaching them how to use these technologies, but also about instilling a sense of responsibility and awareness regarding their financial actions. As digital transactions become more ingrained in our daily lives, it is imperative for the younger generation to be well-versed and prudent in their use. This foundational understanding sets the stage for more responsible and informed financial behaviors as they grow into digitally savvy adults.

The basics of online banking and safety

As the financial world embraces digital technology, online banking has become a staple in managing personal finances. However, with this convenience comes the need for heightened awareness and understanding of online banking safety. This expanded section will delve into the fundamentals of online banking, highlighting its key features, benefits, and crucial safety measures. This knowledge is essential for children to navigate the digital banking landscape securely and confidently.

Understanding Online Banking

1. **What is Online Banking?**: Online banking, also known as internet banking, allows users to conduct financial transactions via the internet. It's a virtual version of a bank that can be accessed on a computer or mobile device.

2. **Key Features of Online Banking**:

- **Account Management**: View account balances, transaction history, and account statements.

- **Fund Transfers**: Transfer money between accounts or to other people.

- **Bill Payments**: Pay bills electronically, set up automatic payments or recurring payments.

- **Mobile Deposits**: Deposit checks using a mobile device by taking a photo of the check.

- **Loan Applications and Management**: Apply for loans and manage them online.

- **Investment Services**: Access to investment accounts and services.

3. **Benefits of Online Banking**:

   - **Convenience and Accessibility**: Bank from anywhere at any time without the need to visit a physical branch.

   - **Efficiency**: Quick and easy transactions, including instant transfers and bill payments.

   - **Real-Time Information**: Up-to-date account information and real-time tracking of transactions.

Online Banking Safety Basics
1. **Secure Internet Connection**: Always use a secure, private Wi-Fi network for online banking. Public Wi-Fi networks can be insecure, making it easier for hackers to access your information.

2. **Strong Passwords and Authentication**: Use strong, unique passwords for banking accounts. Take advantage of multi-factor authentication (MFA) for an additional layer of security.

3. **Regular Monitoring of Accounts**: Encourage regular monitoring of bank accounts for any unauthorized transactions or suspicious activity. Early detection is key to preventing potential fraud.

4. **Phishing Scams Awareness**: Teach about phishing scams where fraudsters attempt to acquire sensitive information such as usernames, passwords, and credit card details. Explain the importance of not clicking on suspicious links or sharing banking details over email or phone.

5. **Software and App Updates**: Keep all devices, applications, and anti-virus software up to date to protect against the latest security threats.

6. **Bank's Security Measures**: Familiarize with the bank's own security measures and protocols. Most banks offer resources to help customers understand how to use their online banking services safely.

7. **Educating on Digital Footprint**: Discuss the importance of a safe digital footprint and how oversharing personal information on social media can lead to security risks, especially in relation to financial information.

In an era where digital transactions are the norm, a solid understanding of online banking and its safety is indispensable. By educating children about the functionalities of online banking and the importance of stringent security practices, they can be better prepared to manage their finances in a digital world. Responsible and secure use of online banking resources is a critical skill for digital-age financial literacy, ensuring that children grow up to be savvy and safe digital consumers.

Teaching kids about cyber security in finance

In the digital age, cyber security is a critical aspect of managing finances. As children become increasingly involved in digital financial activities, it's essential to educate them about the risks and best practices of cyber security in finance. This section will provide comprehensive content on teaching children about the importance of protecting their financial information online, understanding common cyber threats, and adopting safe digital habits. This education is crucial in equipping them with the skills to navigate the digital financial world securely.

Understanding Cyber Security in Finance

1. **What is Cyber Security?**: Explain cyber security as the practice of protecting internet-connected systems, including hardware, software, and data, from digital attacks, theft, and damage.

2. **Importance in Finance**: Emphasize that in finance, cyber security is vital for

protecting money and personal financial information from cybercriminals who can steal identities, access bank accounts, or commit fraud.

Common Cyber Threats in Finance
1. **Phishing Scams**: Teach about phishing attacks where scammers send emails or messages pretending to be a legitimate institution (like a bank) to trick individuals into providing personal and financial information.

2. **Malware and Ransomware**: Explain malware, software designed to harm or exploit any programmable device, and ransomware, a type of malware that locks users out of their devices or data, demanding a ransom.

3. **Identity Theft**: Discuss how cybercriminals can steal personal information to impersonate someone and gain access to their financial resources.

Safe Digital Financial Habits
1. **Strong Passwords**: Teach the importance of creating strong, unique passwords for each online account and changing them regularly.

2. **Secure Networks**: Stress the use of secure, private internet connections for financial transactions. Explain the risks of using public Wi-Fi for banking or shopping.

3. **Recognizing and Reporting Scams**: Educate them on how to recognize suspicious emails or messages and the importance of not clicking on links or downloading attachments from unknown sources. Encourage reporting any suspicious activity to a trusted adult.

4. **Regular Monitoring of Accounts**: Advise them to regularly check bank and online accounts for any unusual activity and report any discrepancies immediately.

5. **Educational Resources and Games**: Utilize online resources, games, and apps designed to teach children about cyber security in a fun and engaging way.

6. **Privacy Settings and Digital Footprint**: Discuss the importance of privacy settings on social media and being cautious about the personal information shared online.

Teaching kids about cyber security in finance is crucial in preparing them to protect themselves in a digital world where financial transactions are increasingly online. By understanding common cyber threats and practicing safe digital habits, children can confidently and securely navigate online financial platforms. This knowledge not only safeguards their current financial interactions but also lays a foundation for secure financial management as they grow into adulthood.

Chapter Six

The Role of Money in Life

Money and Happiness

Money plays a significant role in our lives, but its relationship with happiness is complex and multifaceted. This section explores the value of money in life, the balance between material and non-material sources of happiness, and ways families can appreciate joys that aren't tied to monetary wealth. By understanding this balance, children can develop a more holistic view of happiness and success.

Discussing the value of money in life

To foster a comprehensive understanding of money's role in life, it's crucial to delve into its various dimensions and impacts. This expanded discussion aims to provide a nuanced perspective on how money influences different aspects of our lives, shaping experiences, opportunities, and personal well-being.

Fundamental Roles of Money

1. **Means of Exchange**: Emphasize that money primarily functions as a means of exchange. It simplifies the process of obtaining goods and services, compared to the complexities of a barter system.

2. **Store of Value**: Money serves as a store of value. It allows individuals to save and plan for future needs, whether for emergencies, education, significant life events, or retirement.

3. **Unit of Account**: Explain how money provides a standard measure of value,

making it easier to compare the worth of different goods and services.

Money and Basic Needs

1. **Survival and Security**: Discuss how money is essential for basic survival – purchasing food, securing a home, and accessing healthcare. Explain the concept of financial security and its role in reducing stress and anxiety related to uncertain future needs.

2. **Standard of Living**: Explore how the amount and management of money impact one's standard of living. This includes the quality and accessibility of housing, healthcare, education, and leisure activities.

Money's Psychological and Social Implications

1. **Psychological Impact**: Delve into how financial stability or instability can affect mental health. Financial stress can lead to anxiety and depression, while financial security can contribute to a sense of well-being.

2. **Social Status and Relationships**: Discuss how society often perceives money as a symbol of success and status. Explore how this perception can influence social relationships and self-esteem.

3. **Work-Life Balance**: Money's role in work-life balance is critical. Higher-paying jobs might demand more time and energy, potentially impacting personal and family life.

Money, Opportunities, and Personal Growth

1. **Access to Education and Career Choices**: Money can significantly influence educational opportunities and, consequently, career paths. Higher education and specialized training often require substantial financial investment.

2. **Personal Development**: Highlight how money can facilitate personal growth, such as funding for hobbies, travel, or learning new skills.

3. **Philanthropy and Giving Back**: Discuss how having financial resources can enable individuals to contribute to society, support charities, and aid those in need.

Teaching Responsible Money Management

1. **Budgeting and Saving**: Instill the importance of managing money wisely through budgeting and saving. Teach children to differentiate between needs and wants.

2. **Investing in Experiences**: Encourage investing in experiences, like travel or cultural activities, which can enrich life and create lasting memories, over merely accumulating material possessions.

3. **Ethical Earning and Spending**: Discuss the importance of earning money ethically and spending it in ways that align with one's values and contribute positively to society.

In sum, money is a multifaceted entity with a profound impact on almost every aspect of life. Its value extends beyond mere purchasing power to influence security, opportunities, personal development, and social dynamics. Understanding money's comprehensive role equips individuals, especially children, to navigate their financial journey with awareness, responsibility, and a balanced perspective. It underscores the importance of not only acquiring money but also managing it wisely and ethically for a fulfilling and meaningful life.

Balancing material and non-material happiness

Achieving a balance between material and non-material happiness is essential for a well-rounded and fulfilling life. This expanded discussion will delve into the nuances of finding harmony between the joy derived from material possessions and the contentment found in non-material aspects of life. We'll explore strategies to maintain this balance and ways to instill these values in children.

Understanding Material Happiness

1. **The Role of Material Possessions**: Acknowledge that material possessions, such as toys, gadgets, clothes, and other goods, can bring joy and convenience. They often represent rewards for hard work and can enhance the quality of life.

2. **Limitations of Materialism**: Discuss how material possessions offer temporary satisfaction. The initial excitement often fades, leading to a cycle of continuous desire for more or newer items, which can detract from long-term happiness.

3. **Consumer Culture and Impact**: Explore the impact of living in a con-

sumer-driven society, where success and happiness are often measured by material wealth, and how this perception can skew priorities.

Embracing Non-Material Happiness

1. **Relationships and Connections**: Highlight the importance of relationships with family, friends, and community. Strong social connections are key to long-term happiness and fulfillment.

2. **Personal Growth and Self-Realization**: Encourage pursuits that lead to personal growth, such as education, hobbies, sports, arts, and spiritual practices. These endeavors often provide deeper and more lasting satisfaction than material possessions.

3. **Experiences Over Things**: Stress the value of experiences – travel, cultural activities, adventure sports, volunteering – that enrich life and create lasting memories.

4. **Health and Well-being**: Emphasize the importance of physical, mental, and emotional health as foundational elements of non-material happiness.

Balancing Strategies

1. **Gratitude Practice**: Cultivate a habit of gratitude. Regularly acknowledging and appreciating what one has – both material and non-material – can shift focus from what's lacking to what's abundant.

2. **Mindful Consumption**: Encourage thoughtful and intentional purchasing. This involves buying things that are truly needed or will genuinely enhance life, rather than impulsive or status-driven shopping.

3. **Quality over Quantity**: Teach the principle of valuing quality over quantity in material possessions. Choosing fewer but better-quality items can lead to more satisfaction and less clutter.

4. **Setting Priorities**: Help children understand how to prioritize non-material aspects like family time, personal achievements, and experiences. Discuss setting goals and making choices that reflect these priorities.

Family Activities to Reinforce the Balance

1. **Family Discussions and Reflections**: Have open discussions about happiness, what it means to each family member, and how different activities or possessions contribute to it.

2. **Volunteering Together**: Engage in community service as a family. This can demonstrate the joy of helping others and the fulfillment derived from non-materialistic pursuits.

3. **Nature Activities**: Spend time in nature – hiking, camping, or just playing in a park – to appreciate the simple joys that the natural world offers.

4. **Sharing and Storytelling**: Encourage sharing stories about personal experiences, family history, and life lessons that emphasize values, relationships, and personal growth.

Balancing material and non-material happiness is about understanding the role of each in our lives and making conscious choices that align with our values and true sources of fulfillment. By teaching children to find joy in both material possessions and non-material experiences, we guide them towards a more balanced, content, and meaningful life. This balance is key to nurturing well-rounded individuals who appreciate the full spectrum of what life has to offer.

Family activities to appreciate non-material joys

Cultivating an appreciation for non-material joys is crucial for a well-balanced and fulfilling life. Engaging in family activities that emphasize non-materialistic values can be a powerful way to teach children about the joys that don't come with a price tag. This expanded section provides a range of activities that families can undertake to celebrate and appreciate the non-material aspects of happiness.

1. Nature-Based Activities
- **Outdoor Adventures**: Plan regular outings like hikes, nature walks, or beach days. These activities offer a chance to connect with the natural world and appreciate its beauty, fostering a sense of awe and contentment.

- **Gardening Together**: Start a family garden. Gardening is a rewarding activity that teaches patience, care, and the satisfaction of nurturing growth.

2. Creative and Artistic Pursuits
- **Family Art Projects**: Engage in collective art projects like painting a mural,

creating a family scrapbook, or crafting together. These activities emphasize creativity and expression over material gain.

- **Music and Dance**: Share music and dance as a family. Whether it's playing instruments together, attending a community concert, or having a dance-off in the living room, these activities bring joy and strengthen bonds.

3. Volunteering and Community Service

- **Community Projects**: Participate in local community service projects like food drives, park clean-ups, or volunteering at a shelter. These activities teach compassion and the value of contributing to the community.

- **Helping Neighbors**: As a family, offer help to neighbors or friends in need. This could be as simple as helping with gardening, running errands for the elderly, or organizing a community event.

4. Intellectual and Educational Activities

- **Family Book Club**: Start a family book club where everyone reads the same book and discusses it. This encourages a love for reading and deepens understanding through discussion.

- **Educational Games and Puzzles**: Engage in educational games, puzzles, or building projects that challenge the mind and promote problem-solving skills.

5. Mindfulness and Wellness Activities

- **Family Yoga or Meditation**: Practice yoga or meditation together. These practices promote mental and physical well-being and teach the value of inner peace.

- **Cooking Healthy Meals**: Cook and enjoy healthy meals as a family. This not only teaches valuable life skills but also emphasizes the importance of health and well-being.

6. Storytelling and Sharing Experiences

- **Sharing Personal Stories**: Allocate time for family members to share stories about their life experiences, lessons learned, or family history. This fosters a sense of connection and belonging.

- **Gratitude Sessions**: Regularly share what each person is grateful for. This can be done during dinner or as a separate family ritual, highlighting the joys and blessings in life.

7. Simple Pleasures and Traditions
- **Stargazing Nights**: Spend a night stargazing, talking about the universe, and reflecting on life's wonders.
- **Establishing Family Traditions**: Create your own family traditions, like weekend breakfasts, annual camping trips, or holiday crafts, that become cherished, non-materialistic memories.

Through these varied activities, families can deeply appreciate the richness of life that goes beyond material possessions. Such experiences not only bring joy and fulfillment but also instill in children the understanding that happiness can be found in simple pleasures, relationships, personal growth, and contributing to the greater good. These non-material joys are fundamental to a well-rounded and contented life, teaching children the value of experiences and connections over material wealth.

5.2 Sharing and Caring

Sharing and caring are fundamental values that contribute to the development of empathy, compassion, and community spirit. In this section, we'll explore the importance of sharing with others, practical ways to cultivate generosity, and the positive impact that giving can have on the community. By teaching these principles, children learn to value and practice kindness, leading to a more harmonious and supportive society.

The importance of sharing with others

Sharing is a fundamental social skill that plays a crucial role in building relationships, communities, and empathetic individuals. It's more than just a childhood lesson; it's a lifelong practice that enriches both the giver and the recipient. This expanded section delves deeper into why sharing is essential, its benefits for personal development, and its impact on society.

1. Building Empathy and Emotional Intelligence
- **Understanding Others**: Sharing helps children understand and respond to the feelings and needs of others. It fosters emotional intelligence, a key factor in developing strong, healthy relationships.
- **Developing Compassion**: Regular acts of sharing cultivate compassion and

kindness. It teaches children to care about the well-being of others and to act selflessly.

2. **Enhancing Social Skills and Relationships**
   - **Social Bonding**: Sharing activities encourage interactions and cooperation among peers, strengthening social bonds and friendships.
   - **Conflict Resolution**: Learning to share can also be a valuable lesson in managing conflicts and negotiating solutions, important skills in both childhood and adulthood.

3. **Fostering a Sense of Community and Belonging**
   - **Community Spirit**: Sharing within a community, be it a school, neighborhood, or larger society, fosters a sense of belonging and collective well-being.
   - **Role in Society**: Teaching children the importance of sharing instills a sense of responsibility towards their community and society, highlighting their role in supporting and uplifting others.

4. **Personal Development and Satisfaction**
   - **Self-esteem and Confidence**: Sharing can boost self-esteem and confidence. Children feel good about themselves when they help others, reinforcing positive self-perception.
   - **Moral and Ethical Growth**: It also contributes to moral and ethical development. Understanding the joy of giving can shape a child's values and attitudes towards life.

5. **Preparing for Future Life Situations**
   - **Adulthood Preparation**: The practice of sharing prepares children for future life situations where teamwork, cooperation, and generosity are essential.
   - **Workplace Skills**: In professional settings, the ability to share ideas, time, and resources is invaluable. Early lessons in sharing can lay the foundation for effective teamwork and collaboration skills.

6. **Global Perspective and Understanding**
   - **Cultural Awareness**: Sharing experiences can also lead to a greater understand-

ing of diverse cultures and backgrounds, promoting inclusivity and tolerance.

- **Global Citizenship**: It helps children see themselves as part of a larger global community, where sharing and cooperation can lead to positive change on a broader scale.

In summary, the act of sharing is much more than a simple social transaction; it's a vital component of human interaction and personal development. By emphasizing the importance of sharing with others, we equip children with essential life skills. These skills include empathy, cooperation, social responsibility, and a sense of global citizenship, all of which are crucial for their growth into well-rounded, compassionate adults. The lessons learned from sharing resonate far beyond childhood, influencing one's approach to life and relationships in profound ways.

Simple ways to practice generosity

Generosity is a virtue that can be nurtured from a young age. Practicing generosity doesn't always mean grand gestures; often, it's the small acts of kindness that make a significant impact. This expanded section provides practical and simple ways for families to incorporate generosity into their daily lives, fostering a spirit of giving and kindness in children.

1. Sharing Within the Home

- **Toy and Clothes Sharing**: Encourage children to share toys and clothes with siblings or friends. This could include passing on items they no longer use to those who need them.

- **Chore Sharing**: Implement a system where family members take turns or help each other with household chores, teaching the value of helping and working together.

2. Community Involvement

- **Participate in Local Events**: Engage in community events that focus on giving back, like charity runs, food drives, or community gardening.

- **Neighborhood Assistance**: Offer help to neighbors, such as assisting elderly residents with grocery shopping or lawn care.

3. Acts of Kindness

- **Random Acts of Kindness**: Encourage children to perform simple acts of kindness, such as writing appreciation notes, helping a classmate with schoolwork, or sharing a snack.

- **Kindness Jar**: Create a 'kindness jar' where family members can write down acts of kindness they've done or experienced each week, fostering an awareness of daily generosity.

4. Charitable Actions
- **Donating to Charity**: Involve children in the process of selecting and donating to charities. This could be through monetary donations or giving away toys, books, and clothes.

- **Volunteering Time**: Spend time volunteering at local shelters, food banks, or non-profit organizations. This can be a powerful experience for children to see the impact of their efforts.

5. Teaching Gratitude
- **Gratitude Journal**: Maintain a family gratitude journal where everyone can note things they're thankful for, emphasizing the importance of appreciating what they have.

- **Thank You Notes**: Encourage writing thank you notes for gifts received or for acts of kindness, fostering a habit of acknowledging and appreciating others' generosity.

6. Supporting Causes
- **Fundraising for Causes**: Support causes that your family cares about by participating in or organizing fundraising activities like bake sales or car washes.

- **Educational Awareness**: Educate children about global issues and how their actions, even as small as conserving water or recycling, contribute to a larger cause.

7. Incorporating Generosity in Celebrations
- **Gift-Giving**: During holidays or birthdays, involve children in choosing and preparing gifts for family members, friends, and those in need.

- **Celebration Donations**: On special occasions, consider donating to a charity instead of or in addition to traditional celebrations.

By practicing these simple yet meaningful acts of generosity, children learn the joy and importance of giving. These activities not only foster a culture of kindness and empathy within the family but also contribute to building a compassionate and caring community. Generosity enriches both the giver and the receiver, creating a more connected and supportive society.

The impact of giving on the community

The act of giving, whether in the form of time, resources, or skills, can have a profound and far-reaching impact on communities. This expanded discussion aims to shed light on how generosity can transform both the giver and the receiver, fostering a sense of unity and promoting positive change in the community. We'll explore various aspects of giving's impact and how it contributes to the overall health and well-being of a community.

1. **Strengthening Community Bonds**
   - **Fostering Cooperation and Trust**: Acts of giving within a community build a sense of trust and cooperation among its members. When people see others contributing to the common good, it often inspires them to do the same, creating a cycle of generosity.

   - **Creating Connections**: Volunteer activities and community projects bring people together, often bridging gaps across age groups, cultures, and socioeconomic backgrounds. These interactions can lead to stronger, more cohesive communities.

2. **Enhancing Quality of Life**
   - **Direct Support to Those in Need**: Donations and volunteering directly support individuals and families in need, providing essential resources like food, clothing, and shelter, and improving their quality of life.

   - **Improving Community Resources**: Contributions can lead to improved community resources, such as better schools, parks, and public services, which benefit everyone in the community.

3. **Promoting Community Health and Well-being**
   - **Mental Health Benefits**: Communities with a strong culture of giving tend to have members with better mental health. The act of giving can reduce stress,

combat depression, and increase overall happiness.

- **Encouraging Healthy Behaviors**: Community health initiatives supported by volunteers and donations can promote healthier lifestyles, contributing to the physical well-being of community members.

4. **Economic Benefits**
   - **Supporting Local Economies**: When people donate to local charities and non-profits, they help support jobs and services that are crucial to the local economy.

   - **Cultivating a Philanthropic Culture**: A community that actively engages in giving can attract more resources, investments, and services, further stimulating local economic growth.

5. **Educational Impact**
   - **Learning and Skill Development**: Community-based educational programs, often funded by donations and run by volunteers, can offer valuable learning opportunities and skill development for children and adults alike.

   - **Raising Social Awareness**: Participatory giving activities can raise awareness about social issues and challenges within the community, leading to more informed and engaged citizens.

6. **Long-Term Community Development**
   - **Sustainable Changes**: Sustained giving can lead to long-term improvements in the community, such as poverty reduction, increased access to education, and environmental sustainability.

   - **Inspiring Future Generations**: Demonstrating the value of giving instills a sense of responsibility and altruism in younger generations, ensuring the continuation of community support and development.

The impact of giving on a community is both immediate and long-lasting. It transcends mere material assistance, fostering a sense of belonging, shared responsibility, and mutual respect. The benefits of giving ripple through communities, touching lives and inspiring positive change. When communities embrace the spirit of generosity, they lay the foundation for a more supportive, resilient, and prosperous society.

5.3 Financial Independence

Financial independence is a critical life skill, and introducing its concepts to children can set the foundation for a responsible and self-reliant future. This section delves into the steps towards achieving financial independence for kids, how to encourage responsibility and self-reliance in financial matters, and the importance of celebrating milestones in their journey towards financial autonomy.

Steps towards financial independence for kids

Teaching kids about financial independence involves guiding them through a series of steps that build their understanding, skills, and habits around money management. This detailed exploration provides a structured approach to fostering financial independence in children, which is crucial for their future financial security and success.

1. **Basic Financial Education**
   - **Understanding Money**: Begin with the basics of what money is, how it is earned, and its value. Use real-life examples to make the concepts relatable.

   - **Introduction to Budgeting**: Teach them how to budget their allowances or earnings from small jobs. Show them how to track their income and plan their spending.

2. **Earning Money**
   - **Allowances for Chores**: Implement a system where children can earn their allowance by completing household chores. This ties the concept of work to money.

   - **Small Jobs and Ventures**: Encourage older kids to take on small jobs like babysitting, pet sitting, or lawn mowing. They could also start a mini-business like a lemonade stand or selling crafts.

3. **Saving and Goal Setting**
   - **Opening a Savings Account**: Help them open a savings account and explain how it works, including the concept of interest.

   - **Setting Savings Goals**: Encourage them to set achievable savings goals, whether it's buying a toy, saving for a larger purchase, or setting aside money for future use.

4. Smart Spending
- **Needs vs. Wants**: Teach them to distinguish between needs (essentials) and wants (luxuries), helping them make informed spending decisions.

- **Comparative Shopping**: Show them how to compare prices and look for deals to get the most value for their money.

5. Investing Basics
- **Simple Investment Concepts**: For older children, introduce basic investment concepts. Explain stocks, bonds, and simple savings instruments like fixed deposits or savings bonds.

- **Practical Experience**: Use online simulations or games that teach investment basics in a kid-friendly manner.

6. Understanding Credit
- **Credit Cards and Loans**: Discuss how credit cards and loans work. Emphasize the importance of borrowing responsibly and the concept of interest on borrowed money.

7. Philanthropy and Giving
- **Importance of Giving**: Teach the importance of giving and sharing with others. Encourage them to allocate a portion of their savings for charitable causes.

8. Financial Decision-Making Skills
- **Involvement in Family Finances**: Involve them in simple family financial decisions, such as planning a budget for a family event or comparing prices during grocery shopping.

- **Learning from Financial Decisions**: Allow them to make small financial decisions and learn from both successes and mistakes.

9. Advanced Financial Management (for Teenagers)
- **Budget Management**: Guide them in managing a more complex budget, perhaps for their school expenses or a personal project.

- **Long-Term Financial Planning**: Introduce the concept of long-term financial planning, including saving for college, a car, or other significant future expenses.

The journey towards financial independence is gradual and requires consistent guidance and practice. By teaching kids these essential steps, they develop a solid foundation in money management, decision-making, and financial responsibility. These skills are invaluable as they grow into adults who can confidently navigate the complexities of personal finance. Celebrating each step they master not only reinforces their learning but also builds their confidence in managing financial matters independently.

Encouraging responsibility and self-reliance

Developing responsibility and self-reliance in children is essential for their growth into capable and independent adults. This expanded section will provide detailed strategies and activities to help children learn and practice these vital skills, particularly in the realm of personal and financial management.

1. Responsibility through Daily Routines
- **Chore Systems**: Implement a system where children are responsible for certain chores around the house. This could include tasks like setting the table, cleaning their room, or taking care of a pet.

- **Routine Management**: Encourage children to manage their daily routines, such as homework, study time, and extracurricular activities, fostering time management skills.

2. Financial Responsibility
- **Budgeting Practice**: Teach children to create and manage a simple budget for their allowances or earnings. Include categories for saving, spending, and giving.

- **Earned Allowances**: Link allowances to chores or tasks, showing that money is earned. This teaches the value of hard work and money management.

3. Decision-Making and Problem Solving
- **Guided Choices**: Provide opportunities for children to make choices, such as selecting clothes, planning a meal, or deciding how to spend their free time.

- **Problem-Solving Scenarios**: Present them with age-appropriate problems and guide them through the process of finding solutions, enhancing their critical thinking skills.

4. **Independence in Learning and Projects**
   - **Homework Independence**: Encourage children to tackle their homework independently, offering help only when necessary. This builds study skills and personal responsibility.

   - **Individual Projects**: Motivate them to take on individual projects, such as a science fair project or a personal hobby, guiding them to plan and execute it on their own.

5. **Financial Education and Experiences**
   - **Savings Accounts**: Help them open a savings account and teach them how to manage it, including making deposits and understanding interest.

   - **Shopping Involvement**: Involve children in grocery shopping or other purchasing decisions, teaching them to compare prices, budget, and understand the value of money.

6. **Emotional Self-Reliance**
   - **Handling Emotions**: Teach children to understand and manage their emotions. Encourage them to express their feelings and discuss ways to handle challenging situations.

   - **Self-Care Skills**: Promote self-care skills, such as personal hygiene, basic cooking, and laundry, preparing them for independent living.

7. **Modeling and Mentorship**
   - **Lead by Example**: Demonstrate responsibility and self-reliance in your actions. Children often learn by observing adults.

   - **Share Stories**: Share stories of your experiences where you had to be responsible and self-reliant, including both successes and challenges.

8. **Encouraging Community Participation**
   - **Volunteer Work**: Involve children in volunteer work or community service projects, which can teach the importance of being responsible members of a community.

   - **Group Activities and Team Sports**: Encourage participation in group activities or team sports where children learn to cooperate, contribute, and depend on their skills.

Fostering responsibility and self-reliance is a multifaceted approach that requires consistent effort and guidance. By providing opportunities for children to make decisions, manage finances, solve problems, and take charge of their daily activities, they develop a strong sense of independence. These skills are invaluable and lay the groundwork for success in various aspects of life, including personal development, academic achievement, and future financial stability.

Celebrating independence milestones

Recognizing and celebrating milestones in a child's journey towards independence is crucial for reinforcing their growth and achievements. These celebrations can range from small acknowledgments to family traditions, each marking an important step in their development. This detailed exploration provides ideas on how to celebrate various independence milestones, emphasizing their significance in a child's growth and self-reliance.

1. **Financial Milestones**
   - **First Savings Goal Achieved**: Celebrate when a child reaches their first savings goal. This could involve a special acknowledgment during a family dinner, a small reward, or an experience they enjoy.

   - **Opening Their First Bank Account**: Make the opening of their first bank account a significant event. Perhaps mark it with a special outing or a ceremonial deposit to their new account.

   - **Making Their First Purchase with Earned Money**: When a child makes their first purchase with money they've earned themselves, celebrate this as a step towards financial independence. Discuss with them the sense of achievement and responsibility that comes with it.

2. **Personal Development Milestones**
   - **Learning a New Skill**: Whether it's riding a bike, cooking a meal, or learning a musical instrument, celebrate these new skills as steps towards self-reliance.

   - **Overcoming a Personal Challenge**: Acknowledge when a child overcomes a personal challenge, such as dealing with a fear or resolving a conflict independently.

3. **Academic and Extracurricular Achievements**
   - **School Milestones**: Celebrate academic milestones like moving up a grade, excelling in a subject, or completing a challenging project.
   - **Extracurricular Accomplishments**: Acknowledge achievements in extracurricular activities like sports, arts, or community service.

4. **Emotional and Social Milestones**
   - **Handling a Difficult Situation**: Commend them when they handle a difficult or uncomfortable situation well, like resolving a dispute with a friend or managing a disappointment.
   - **Demonstrating Empathy and Kindness**: Recognize moments when they show significant empathy and kindness, as these are important aspects of emotional independence.

5. **Household and Family Contributions**
   - **Contributing to Household Chores**: Recognize their regular contributions to household chores as part of becoming a responsible family member.
   - **Caring for Siblings or Family Members**: Celebrate instances where they show responsibility in caring for younger siblings or assisting family members.

6. **Personal Care and Responsibility**
   - **Self-Care Routines**: When a child starts taking charge of their personal care routines, acknowledge this as an important step towards independence.
   - **Time Management and Organization**: Recognize their efforts in managing their time effectively for school work, chores, and other activities.

7. **Creative Celebrations**
   - **Independence Day**: Establish an annual 'Independence Day' to celebrate milestones achieved throughout the year.
   - **Milestone Board or Journal**: Keep a family milestone board or a journal where these achievements are recorded and celebrated.

Celebrating independence milestones is about more than just acknowledging achievements; it's about reinforcing a child's sense of self-worth, capability, and progress in becoming independent. These celebrations help instill confidence and pride in their abilities and motivate them to continue striving towards greater independence. By recognizing these milestones, families can foster an environment where growth is celebrated, and each step towards independence is valued.

5.4 Money and Relationships

Discussing money in family and with friends

Money is often considered a taboo subject in many social contexts, yet it's a crucial aspect of life that can affect personal relationships. Discussing money matters openly and respectfully within the family and with friends is key to maintaining healthy relationships. This expanded discussion offers insights and strategies on how to approach money talks in a comfortable and constructive manner.

1. Discussing Money Within the Family

- **Regular Family Finance Meetings**: Establish a routine of having regular family discussions about finances. This can include budgeting, saving for goals, and any financial challenges.

- **Involving Children in Financial Planning**: Include children in age-appropriate financial discussions. This could involve planning for a family vacation, discussing savings goals, or explaining household bills.

- **Setting Financial Goals Together**: Work as a family to set financial goals. This could be saving for a shared family experience or a long-term goal like college funds or home improvements.

- **Transparency and Honesty**: Be transparent about financial situations, including challenges. This helps in building trust and understanding within the family.

2. Money Conversations with Friends

- **Sensitivity and Tact**: Approach money discussions with friends sensitively. Be aware of differing financial backgrounds and avoid topics that might be uncomfortable.

- **Splitting Expenses**: When it comes to shared expenses, such as during outings or trips, discuss openly how costs will be divided. Consider using apps that can help manage and split expenses fairly.

- **Lending and Borrowing Money**: If lending or borrowing money between friends, be clear about the terms and expectations to avoid misunderstandings.

- **Respecting Privacy**: Understand and respect each other's privacy regarding financial matters. Avoid prying into personal financial details unless openly shared.

3. Navigating Financial Peer Pressure
- **Teaching Children about Peer Influence**: Educate children about peer pressure related to money, such as the urge to spend on trends or activities they can't afford.

- **Encouraging Smart Spending**: Discuss how to make smart spending choices and not be influenced by what others are buying or spending.

4. Modeling Positive Money Talks
- **Lead by Example**: Model positive money discussions as adults. Show children and peers that it's okay to talk about finances in a constructive and non-judgmental way.

- **Conflict Resolution in Financial Matters**: Demonstrate how to resolve financial conflicts calmly and rationally, emphasizing communication and understanding.

5. Cultural and Personal Sensitivities
- **Understanding Cultural Differences**: Recognize that cultural backgrounds can influence attitudes towards money. Be respectful and considerate of these differences in discussions.

- **Individual Financial Values**: Acknowledge that everyone has different financial values and priorities. Respect these differences while sharing your perspectives.

Open and respectful discussions about money in family and social circles are essential for fostering understanding and preventing conflicts. By practicing transparency, sensitivity, and good communication skills, these discussions can strengthen relationships rather than strain them. It's important to create an environment where financial matters are approached with honesty, respect, and a willingness to understand different perspectives.

Simple ways to handle money disagreements

Money disagreements, whether within the family or between friends, are common, but how they're handled can significantly affect relationships. It's essential to navigate these conflicts with understanding, communication, and respect. This expanded section provides detailed strategies to effectively manage and resolve money disagreements in a constructive manner.

1. Open and Honest Communication

- **Encourage Open Discussion**: Create an environment where each party feels comfortable expressing their views on the financial matter at hand. Open communication is key to understanding each other's perspectives.

- **Active Listening**: Practice active listening. This means genuinely paying attention to the other person's viewpoint without immediately thinking of a response or rebuttal.

2. Identify the Root Cause

- **Understand the Underlying Issues**: Often, money disagreements are symptoms of deeper issues, such as differences in values or financial insecurity. Identifying the real issue can lead to more effective solutions.

- **Acknowledge Emotions**: Recognize and acknowledge the emotions involved in financial disagreements. Money can often trigger strong feelings like stress, frustration, or insecurity.

3. Seeking Compromise and Collaboration

- **Finding Common Ground**: Look for areas of agreement and build from there. Finding even small commonalities can pave the way for compromise.

- **Collaborative Problem-Solving**: Approach the disagreement with a problem-solving mindset. Work together to find solutions that meet both parties' needs and concerns.

4. Setting Clear Financial Boundaries and Expectations

- **Establish Boundaries**: Clearly define financial boundaries and responsibilities. This could include setting limits on shared expenses or agreeing on a budget.

- **Clear Expectations**: Be clear about financial expectations, especially in shared commitments like bills, rent, or loans.

5. Avoiding Blame and Judgment

- **Focus on Solutions, Not Blame**: Concentrate on finding solutions rather than assigning blame. Blaming can escalate the conflict and hinder resolution.

- **Respectful Dialogue**: Maintain a respectful tone even when you disagree. Avoid judgmental language and accusations.

6. Taking Time to Cool Off

- **Pause if Needed**: If the discussion becomes too heated, it's okay to take a break and revisit the conversation later. This can prevent saying things in the heat of the moment that might be regretted later.

7. Seeking External Advice

- **Professional Advice**: In some cases, it might be helpful to seek advice from a financial advisor, especially for more complex financial disagreements.

- **Mediation**: For unresolved conflicts, consider mediation from a neutral third party. This can be particularly useful in situations where emotions are running high.

8. Reflect and Learn from the Experience

- **Post-Conflict Reflection**: After resolving the disagreement, reflect on what was learned from the experience and how similar situations can be handled better in the future.

- **Continuous Financial Education**: Use disagreements as opportunities for learning and improving financial literacy, both individually and collectively.

Handling money disagreements effectively is about more than just reaching a resolution; it's about maintaining healthy relationships and fostering mutual understanding. By employing open communication, empathy, compromise, and respect, it's possible to navigate these disagreements constructively. Remember, the goal is to find solutions that respect everyone's needs and viewpoints, thereby strengthening the relationship and building financial harmony.

Learning to respect different money views

Money, being a deeply personal and often culturally influenced aspect of life, can be viewed and managed in various ways. Understanding and respecting different financial perspectives is crucial in personal interactions and relationships. This expanded section delves into how to cultivate an appreciation for diverse money views, whether within the family, among friends, or in broader social interactions.

1. Recognizing the Diversity of Financial Backgrounds

- **Understand Different Backgrounds**: Acknowledge that financial habits and attitudes are often shaped by one's upbringing, culture, and personal experiences. This diversity can lead to varying views on saving, spending, and investing.

- **Educational Diversity**: Recognize that financial literacy levels can vary greatly. Some individuals may have had more education or exposure to financial planning than others.

2. Empathy and Open-mindedness

- **Practicing Empathy**: Try to put yourself in the other person's shoes to understand their financial perspective. Empathy is key to respect and understanding.

- **Maintaining Open-mindedness**: Approach financial discussions with an open mind. Be willing to listen and learn from others' experiences and viewpoints.

3. Healthy Discussions About Money

- **Constructive Conversations**: Engage in conversations about money that are constructive and informative, rather than confrontational or judgmental.

- **Sharing Knowledge**: Share your own knowledge and experiences with money in a way that is helpful, not imposing. This can be a way to learn from each other.

4. Respecting Financial Privacy

- **Privacy and Boundaries**: Understand and respect individuals' privacy regarding their financial matters. Avoid prying into personal financial details unless willingly shared.

- **Non-Judgmental Approach**: Refrain from judging others based on their financial status, decisions, or habits.

5. Handling Disagreements Respectfully

- **Agreeing to Disagree**: It's okay to have different financial opinions. Agreeing to disagree can be a respectful way to handle divergent views.

- **Finding Common Ground**: In discussions, look for areas of common interest or agreement that can lead to a mutual understanding.

6. Role of Communication in Financial Relationships

- **Effective Communication Skills**: Develop and practice effective communication skills, especially active listening, when discussing financial matters.

- **Expressing Views Diplomatically**: Learn to express your financial views and decisions diplomatically, especially in situations involving shared finances or investments.

7. Learning from Diverse Perspectives

- **Broadening Understanding**: Use opportunities to learn from others' financial perspectives to broaden your own understanding of money management.

- **Adapting and Evolving**: Be open to adapting your financial habits and strategies as you learn from others, whether it's new ways of budgeting, saving, or investing.

8. Cultivating Financial Inclusivity

- **Inclusive Discussions**: Ensure that financial discussions are inclusive, allowing all voices and perspectives to be heard and considered.

- **Respecting Cultural Differences**: Be mindful of cultural differences in financial practices and attitudes. Respect these differences as part of a broader financial inclusivity.

Respecting different money views is fundamental to healthy financial coexistence and relationships. It involves recognizing the diversity of financial backgrounds, practicing empathy, engaging in open and respectful discussions, and maintaining privacy and boundaries. By appreciating and learning from various financial perspectives, individuals can enrich their understanding and approach to money management, leading to more harmonious and mutually respectful financial interactions.

5.5 A Balanced Money Mindset

Developing a healthy attitude towards money

Fostering a healthy attitude towards money is fundamental to achieving financial well-being and overall life satisfaction. It involves creating a balanced view of finances, understanding both its value and limitations. This expanded section provides deeper insights and practical steps to guide children and adults in developing a positive and balanced relationship with money.

1. Understanding Money's True Value

- **Tool for Living**: Emphasize that money is a tool that facilitates various aspects of life, such as education, comfort, and security, but it is not the sole determinant of happiness or success.

- **Limitations of Wealth**: Discuss the limitations of money, acknowledging that it cannot buy love, happiness, or replace the value of experiences and relationships.

2. Avoiding Materialism

- **Focus on Experiences**: Encourage a focus on life experiences over material possessions. Experiences, such as family vacations, educational pursuits, or hobbies, often provide longer-lasting satisfaction than physical items.

- **Critical View of Consumer Culture**: Teach critical thinking about consumer culture and the constant push to buy more. Discuss the difference between needs and wants, and the concept of living within one's means.

3. Gratitude and Contentment

- **Practicing Gratitude**: Foster a sense of gratitude for what one already has. This could be done through regular family discussions, where members share what they are thankful for.

- **Contentment with Simplicity**: Encourage finding joy in simple pleasures and being content with what one has, rather than always striving for more.

4. Financial Responsibility and Control

- **Budgeting and Planning**: Teach the importance of budgeting and financial planning. Show how managing money wisely can lead to financial freedom and reduced stress.

- **Self-Control and Delayed Gratification**: Cultivate self-control in financial matters. Teach the value of delayed gratification and saving for bigger goals.

5. **Positive Money Conversations**
    - **Open Discussions About Money**: Create an environment where money is an open and positive topic of conversation, removing any stigma or anxiety associated with financial discussions.
    - **Learning from Financial Mistakes**: Frame financial mistakes as learning opportunities. Discuss what went wrong, what could be done differently, and how to improve in the future.

6. **Role Models and Mentoring**
    - **Leading by Example**: Be a role model in terms of how you manage and talk about money. Children often emulate the financial habits and attitudes of their parents or guardians.
    - **Mentors and Financial Education**: Encourage learning from mentors or through financial education programs that promote healthy financial habits and attitudes.

7. **Philanthropy and Giving Back**
    - **Importance of Giving**: Teach the importance of giving back, whether it's donating to charity, volunteering time, or helping those in need. This reinforces the message that money can be used to make a positive impact on others' lives.

Developing a healthy attitude towards money is about creating a balanced perspective where financial stability is sought, but not at the expense of life's other valuable aspects. It's about understanding money's role as a facilitator of goals and comfort, practicing gratitude, learning financial responsibility, and using wealth as a means to contribute positively to society. This balanced approach leads to not just financial health but also contributes to overall well-being and life satisfaction.

Positive money affirmations and beliefs

Positive money affirmations and beliefs can significantly influence one's financial behavior and attitudes. By fostering a positive relationship with money, individuals can develop healthier financial habits, reduce anxiety around finances, and work towards financial goals with a more optimistic outlook. This detailed guide explores how to incorporate positive money affirmations and beliefs into everyday life, shaping a constructive and empowering financial mindset.

1. **The Power of Positive Affirmations**
   - **Affirmations for Abundance**: Encourage affirmations that focus on abundance and prosperity, such as "I am open to financial abundance" or "Wealth flows to me in unexpected ways."

   - **Confidence in Financial Management**: Use affirmations that build confidence in managing finances, like "I am capable of making smart financial decisions" or "I wisely manage my financial resources."

2. **Creating a Positive Financial Identity**
   - **Self-Perception and Money**: Develop a self-perception that is aligned with being responsible and successful with money. Affirmations like "I am financially savvy and responsible" can reinforce this identity.

   - **Overcoming Negative Beliefs**: Identify and challenge any negative beliefs about money, replacing them with positive and realistic views. For example, change "I'm just not good with money" to "I am learning and improving my financial skills every day."

3. **Fostering a Growth Mindset Towards Wealth**
   - **Belief in Financial Improvement**: Cultivate a belief that financial situations can improve with effort and smart strategies. An affirmation could be "I am constantly improving my financial situation."

   - **Embracing Financial Learning**: Encourage the belief that learning about finances is an ongoing process, with affirmations like "I am always open to new knowledge and strategies about money management."

4. **Visualizing Financial Goals and Success**
   - **Positive Visualization**: Practice visualizing financial goals as already achieved, which can enhance motivation and the emotional drive to achieve these goals.

- **Affirmations for Goals**: Use specific affirmations related to personal financial goals, such as "I am saving diligently towards buying my first home" or "I am creating a prosperous future for my family."

5. **Gratitude for Current Financial State**
   - **Appreciating What You Have**: Regularly express gratitude for your current financial state, even if it's not where you want to be yet. An affirmation could be "I am thankful for my ability to manage my finances in the present moment."
   - **Recognizing Opportunities**: Affirm the ability to recognize and capitalize on financial opportunities with affirmations like "I see and seize opportunities for financial growth."

6. **Integrating Affirmations into Daily Life**
   - **Daily Affirmation Practice**: Incorporate affirmations into daily routines, such as saying them during morning rituals, writing them in a journal, or using them as reminders throughout the day.
   - **Family Affirmation Activities**: Engage the whole family in positive money affirmations, perhaps during family meetings or discussions about finances.

Adopting positive money affirmations and beliefs is a powerful tool for transforming one's financial mindset. It's about shifting focus from limitations to possibilities, from anxiety to confidence, and from scarcity to abundance. These positive affirmations and beliefs can lead to more fruitful financial behaviors, healthier financial decisions, and a more optimistic approach to achieving financial goals. They are key to building a positive financial identity that supports both personal growth and financial success.

Stories and examples of a balanced money mindset

Incorporating stories and real-life examples is an effective way to illustrate the principles of a balanced money mindset. These narratives can offer valuable lessons and insights into how to approach financial matters with a healthy, balanced perspective. This expanded section will delve into various stories and examples that highlight the importance of a balanced approach to finances.

1. **Historical Figures and Their Financial Wisdom**
   - **Warren Buffett's Philosophy**: Buffett, known for his immense wealth, emphasizes living modestly and not measuring success by monetary value alone.

His story of living in the same house he bought in 1958, despite being a billionaire, underscores the value he places on simplicity and modesty.

- **Andrew Carnegie's Philanthropy**: Carnegie, one of the wealthiest individuals in history, believed in using wealth for the greater good. His extensive philanthropy, funding libraries and educational institutions, exemplifies a balanced view of using wealth for societal benefit.

2. Modern Examples of Financial Balance

- **Entrepreneurs Balancing Wealth and Purpose**: Highlight stories of entrepreneurs who prioritize both profit and purpose. For instance, the founders of companies with strong ethical missions who have successfully combined profitability with social responsibility.

- **Public Figures Advocating Financial Literacy**: Discuss public figures or celebrities who use their platforms to promote financial literacy and responsible money management, balancing their wealth with a mission to educate others.

3. Personal Stories and Case Studies

- **Family Stories**: Share personal or family stories that demonstrate balanced money management. This could include how saving helped overcome a financial challenge or how prioritizing experiences over material possessions brought joy.

- **Community Members as Role Models**: Highlight stories of individuals in the community known for their wise financial habits. These could be local business owners, teachers, or neighbors who exemplify balanced financial living.

4. Fictional Narratives and Parables

- **Literature and Film**: Use characters from books or films that demonstrate a balanced approach to money. Discuss their decisions and outcomes to illustrate the impact of their financial mindset.

- **Parables and Fables**: Refer to classic parables or fables that teach lessons about money, such as Aesop's Fables, which often carry moral lessons about thrift, the dangers of greed, or the value of hard work.

5. **Contrasting Extreme Financial Behaviors**
   - **Cautionary Tales**: Share stories that contrast balanced financial mindsets with extreme behaviors, such as tales of lottery winners who lost their fortunes due to poor money management, or individuals who found happiness despite modest means.

6. **Documentaries and Biographies**
   - **Real-Life Financial Journeys**: Suggest documentaries or biographies that track the financial journeys of various individuals, showing the consequences of different financial attitudes and decisions.

Stories and real-life examples are powerful tools for illustrating the principles and benefits of a balanced money mindset. They provide tangible, relatable contexts in which the concepts of smart financial management, the value of simplicity, and the importance of using wealth for good can be seen in action. These narratives not only educate but also inspire and guide individuals in cultivating their own balanced approach to finances.

Chapter Seven

Preparing for Big Moments

Saving for College

Saving for college is a significant undertaking that requires planning, foresight, and often, a family-wide effort. This section will explore simplified strategies for college savings, understanding scholarships and grants, and how to make saving for college a collective family goal. The aim is to provide a roadmap for families to effectively prepare for this major educational and financial milestone.

Simplified college savings strategies

Saving for college can seem overwhelming, but with the right strategies, it can be manageable and effective. This detailed guide offers a comprehensive look at simplified and practical approaches to saving for college, helping families navigate this crucial financial goal with greater ease and clarity.

1. **Early and Consistent Saving**
   - **Start as Early as Possible**: Begin saving for college as early as the child's birth. The more time money has to grow, the less you may need to save each month.

   - **Regular Savings Plan**: Set up a regular savings plan, depositing a fixed amount each month into a designated college fund. Even small contributions can accumulate significantly over time.

2. **Utilizing Tax-Advantaged College Savings Accounts**
   - **529 Plans**: Investigate 529 college savings plans, which offer tax benefits. Con-

tributions grow tax-deferred, and withdrawals for qualified education expenses are tax-free.

- **Coverdell Education Savings Accounts (ESA)**: Consider a Coverdell ESA, which also provides tax-free earnings growth and tax-free withdrawals for qualifying educational expenses.

3. Automated Savings Mechanisms
- **Automatic Transfers**: Use automated transfers from your checking to your savings account. Automating savings helps ensure consistency and takes the decision-making out of the process.

- **Payroll Deductions**: Some employers offer payroll deduction options directly into 529 plans or other savings accounts, making the process seamless.

4. High-Interest Savings Accounts and Certificates of Deposit (CDs)
- **High-Yield Savings Accounts**: For short-term or more flexible college savings, high-yield savings accounts can offer better interest rates than regular savings accounts.

- **Certificates of Deposit**: CDs can be a good option for risk-free saving. They typically offer higher interest rates in exchange for locking in funds for a set period.

5. Integrating College Savings into Your Overall Financial Plan
- **Balancing with Other Financial Goals**: Ensure college savings are part of a broader financial plan that includes retirement savings, emergency funds, and other financial goals.

- **Reviewing and Adjusting Contributions**: Regularly review your savings plan and adjust contributions as your financial situation changes or as the child gets closer to college age.

6. Encouraging Contributions from Family and Friends
- **Gift Contributions**: Encourage family members and friends to contribute to your child's college fund in lieu of gifts for birthdays, holidays, and other occasions.

- **Matching Gifts**: If family members are willing, set up a matching gift system where they match a portion of your child's savings.

7. Considering Low-Cost Investment Options
- **Index Funds and ETFs**: If you're investing as part of college savings, consider low-cost index funds or ETFs, which can offer diversified exposure to the market with lower fees.

8. Scholarships and Grants as Part of the Strategy
- **Early Research**: Encourage your child to research and apply for scholarships and grants, which can significantly reduce the amount you need to save.

Adopting simplified and effective college savings strategies can make this daunting task more manageable. By starting early, saving consistently, taking advantage of tax benefits, and integrating college savings into your overall financial plan, you can build a substantial fund over time. Encouraging family contributions and considering low-cost investment options can further enhance these savings efforts. Remember, the key is to start as early as possible and keep the momentum going.

Understanding scholarships and grants

Navigating the world of scholarships and grants is essential for students and families looking to offset college expenses. Understanding how these financial aids work, their types, and how to access them can significantly reduce the financial burden of higher education. This detailed guide provides an in-depth look into scholarships and grants, offering valuable insights for effectively utilizing these resources.

1. What Are Scholarships and Grants?
- **Definition and Differences**: Scholarships are typically merit-based awards given to students for academic, athletic, artistic, or other achievements. Grants, on the other hand, are usually need-based financial aids that don't require repayment and are awarded based on the student's financial situation.

- **Sources**: Both scholarships and grants can come from various sources, including federal and state governments, colleges, universities, private organizations, and non-profits.

2. Types of Scholarships
- **Academic Scholarships**: Awarded based on academic performance, such as

GPA, standardized test scores, and academic achievements.

- **Athletic Scholarships**: Given to students with exceptional skills in sports, often requiring the student to play for the college team.

- **Arts and Talent Scholarships**: For students who excel in the arts, including music, art, drama, and writing.

- **Community Service Scholarships**: Awarded to students with significant contributions to community service and volunteer work.

- **Minority Scholarships**: Aimed at students from certain ethnic, racial, or other minority groups, often designed to promote diversity in education.

3. Finding and Applying for Scholarships

- **Research Early**: Start researching scholarship opportunities well in advance. High school counselors, college financial aid offices, and online scholarship databases are good starting points.

- **Application Process**: Understand the application requirements for each scholarship. This may include essays, letters of recommendation, transcripts, and proof of achievements.

- **Deadlines**: Keep track of application deadlines. Missing a deadline can disqualify even the most qualified applicant.

4. Understanding and Applying for Grants

- **Federal and State Grants**: The most common type of grant is the federal Pell Grant, but many states also offer grants to residents. Eligibility is often based on the family's financial need.

- **Filling Out FAFSA**: To apply for federal grants, as well as many state and institutional grants, students must complete the Free Application for Federal Student Aid (FAFSA).

- **Institutional Grants**: Many colleges offer their own grants to students based on need, merit, or a combination of both. Check with individual colleges for application procedures.

5. Maintaining Scholarship and Grant Eligibility
- **Academic Performance**: Many scholarships and grants require maintaining a certain GPA or continuing involvement in a particular activity or sport.
- **Regular Check-Ins**: Stay informed about any changes in the terms of your scholarships or grants, as these can affect your eligibility.

6. Tips for Successful Applications
- **Personalize Applications**: Tailor each application to highlight why you are a perfect fit for that specific scholarship or grant.
- **Proofread and Review**: Ensure that applications are error-free and submitted with all required documentation.

Understanding scholarships and grants is a crucial step in preparing for college expenses. These forms of financial aid can significantly reduce the cost of higher education and make college more accessible. By starting early, staying organized, and diligently pursuing these opportunities, students can maximize their chances of receiving financial support and lessen the financial burden of college education.

Making college savings a family goal

Turning college savings into a family goal can not only ease the financial burden but also foster a sense of unity and shared purpose. It's a strategy that involves the entire family in the saving process, from planning to execution. This detailed guide provides a comprehensive look at how families can collaboratively approach the goal of saving for college.

1. Establishing the Importance of Education
- **Family Discussions**: Initiate conversations about the importance of higher education and its long-term benefits. Explain how saving for college is an investment in the future.
- **Incorporating Values**: Emphasize values like hard work, dedication, and the importance of planning for the future. Make the connection between these values and the process of saving for college.

2. Setting a Collective Goal
- **Shared Vision**: Work together to set a realistic savings goal. This might include researching the costs of different colleges and determining the amount needed.

- **Involvement of Children**: Involve children in setting the goal. This can include discussions about their interests, potential career paths, and choice of schools.

3. Developing a Savings Plan
- **Budgeting as a Family**: Create a family budget with a line item for college savings. Show how cutting back on certain expenses can increase the amount saved for college.

- **Savings Account**: Open a dedicated college savings account like a 529 plan and involve the children in the process. Explain how the account works and its benefits.

4. Contributing to the Savings
- **Encouraging Children's Contributions**: Motivate children to contribute to their college fund from allowances, gifts, or part-time jobs.

- **Matching Contributions**: Implement a system where parents match the children's contributions to some extent. This not only encourages saving but also teaches about employer match programs they might encounter in the future.

5. Monitoring and Adjusting the Plan
- **Regular Check-Ins**: Have periodic family meetings to review the progress of the college savings goal. Use this time to discuss any adjustments needed in the saving strategy.

- **Celebrating Milestones**: Acknowledge and celebrate when significant savings milestones are reached. This could be a family outing or a small reward.

6. Educating on Financial Literacy
- **Teaching Financial Skills**: Use the process of saving for college as an opportunity to teach children about financial literacy, including budgeting, saving, and the power of compound interest.

- **Role Modeling**: Parents can model good financial behavior, showing the importance of saving, making sacrifices for long-term goals, and being financially responsible.

7. Exploring Additional Funding Options

- **Researching Scholarships and Grants**: Encourage children to research and apply for scholarships and grants as part of the collective effort to fund their education.

- **Understanding Financial Aid**: Discuss the role of financial aid in college funding, including how to apply for and utilize it effectively.

Making college savings a family goal is a comprehensive approach that extends beyond merely setting aside money. It's about instilling values, imparting financial knowledge, and working together towards a common objective. This collective effort not only aids in accumulating the necessary funds but also strengthens the family bond and prepares children with the financial acumen they will need in the future.

6.2 First Big Purchases

Embarking on the journey of making a first big purchase is a significant milestone in anyone's life, be it buying a car, a computer, or other substantial items. This chapter will focus on how to effectively plan and save for such purchases, make informed and smart spending decisions, and learn valuable lessons from these experiences. The goal is to equip individuals, especially young adults, with the necessary tools and knowledge to handle large financial commitments responsibly.

Planning and saving for big purchases

Making a big purchase, whether it's a car, a major appliance, or expensive technology, requires thoughtful planning and disciplined saving. Understanding how to effectively navigate this process is crucial for financial health and achieving long-term goals. This comprehensive guide provides detailed steps and strategies for planning and saving for big-ticket items.

1. Defining the Purchase and Its Necessity

- **Identify the Item**: Clearly define what the big purchase is. Whether it's a necessity or a luxury, knowing exactly what you're saving for helps in creating a focused plan.

- **Assessing Need vs. Want**: Distinguish between what you need and what you want. This assessment helps in prioritizing purchases and avoiding unnecessary financial strain.

2. Research and Price Estimation

- **Comprehensive Market Research**: Conduct thorough research on the item.

Look into different brands, models, and their features to find what best suits your needs.

- **Cost Analysis**: Determine the total cost of the purchase, including any additional expenses like accessories, delivery, installation, or insurance.

3. Setting a Target and Timeline

- **Savings Goal**: Establish a clear savings goal based on the total cost. Consider any potential price changes, like seasonal discounts or model updates, which might affect the cost.

- **Timeline for Saving**: Set a realistic timeline for your purchase. This will determine how much you need to save regularly.

4. Creating a Savings Plan

- **Budget Adjustments**: Review and adjust your current budget to accommodate the new savings goal. Identify areas where you can cut back or reduce expenses.

- **Separate Savings Account**: Open a dedicated savings account for this goal. Keeping these funds separate can reduce the temptation to use the money for other expenses.

5. Saving Strategies

- **Automatic Savings**: Set up automatic transfers to your savings account. Automating this process makes it easier to stay consistent with your savings plan.

- **Incremental Increases**: Consider gradually increasing your savings amount over time, especially if your income increases or you reduce other expenses.

6. Considering Additional Income Sources

- **Side Jobs or Gigs**: Look for opportunities to earn extra income through part-time work, freelancing, or selling items you no longer need.

- **Windfalls and Bonuses**: Allocate any unexpected windfalls, such as tax refunds, bonuses, or gifts, directly to your savings goal.

7. Evaluating Financing Options

- **Understanding Financing**: If considering financing options, thoroughly understand the terms, interest rates, and total cost over time. Compare different financing offers to find the most favorable one.

- **Down Payment Strategy**: If a down payment is required, factor this into your savings plan. A larger down payment can often reduce the amount you need to finance and save money on interest.

8. Monitoring Progress and Adjusting as Needed
- **Regular Review**: Periodically review your savings progress and adjust your plan if necessary. This might involve tightening your budget further or extending your timeline.

- **Staying Flexible**: Be prepared to adapt your plan in response to changes in your financial situation, such as unexpected expenses or changes in income.

Careful planning and disciplined saving are key to successfully managing big purchases. By thoroughly researching, setting clear goals, and diligently following a savings plan, you can make substantial purchases without jeopardizing your financial stability. This process not only helps you acquire what you need or desire but also strengthens your overall financial planning and management skills.

Making smart choices when spending big

Making large purchases often involves significant financial commitment and can impact one's financial health for years to come. Therefore, it's essential to approach these decisions with careful consideration and smart strategies. This expanded guide offers a thorough look into how to make intelligent, well-informed choices when facing substantial financial outlays.

1. Thorough Research and Comparison
- **In-depth Product Research**: Before making a big purchase, thoroughly research the product or service. Understand the features, benefits, and any potential drawbacks.

- **Comparing Options**: Don't settle for the first option you find. Compare different models, brands, or providers to ensure you get the best value for your money.

2. Cost-Benefit Analysis

- **Long-Term Value**: Consider the long-term value of the purchase. It's often worth spending more upfront for an item that will last longer or cost less to maintain.

- **Total Cost of Ownership**: Look beyond the purchase price. Consider additional costs like maintenance, operation costs, insurance, and any potential resale value.

3. Seeking Expert Opinions and Reviews

- **Professional Advice**: For technical or specialized purchases (like electronics, vehicles, or home renovations), seek advice from experts or professionals in the field.

- **Customer Reviews and Testimonials**: Check customer reviews and testimonials to gauge the satisfaction of others who have made similar purchases.

4. Timing the Purchase

- **Seasonal Discounts and Sales**: Be aware of seasonal trends and sales periods when prices may be lower. This can include Black Friday sales, end-of-season clearances, or holiday promotions.

- **Avoiding Impulse Buying**: Resist the temptation to make impulse purchases. Give yourself time to consider the necessity and timing of the purchase.

5. Financing and Payment Strategies

- **Affordable Financing**: If financing the purchase, look for the most affordable options. Compare interest rates, loan terms, and total interest costs.

- **Avoiding High-Interest Debt**: Be cautious of financing options with high-interest rates, such as credit card debt, which can significantly increase the total cost.

6. Planning for the Purchase

- **Budgeting for the Expense**: Make sure the purchase fits into your budget without jeopardizing other financial goals or obligations.

- **Saving for the Purchase**: Whenever possible, save for the purchase in advance to minimize or avoid financing costs.

7. **Reflecting on Need vs. Want**
    - **Evaluating Necessity**: Critically evaluate whether the purchase is a need or a want. Focusing on needs helps in making more financially sound decisions.

    - **Emotional Decision-Making**: Be aware of emotional influences on your spending decisions. Sometimes, waiting a few days before making the purchase can provide a clearer perspective.

8. **Negotiating and Seeking the Best Deal**
    - **Negotiation Skills**: Don't hesitate to negotiate the price, especially for high-value items like cars or home appliances. Even small reductions can make a big difference.

    - **Exploring Offers and Discounts**: Look for special offers, discounts, or bundles that provide additional value.

Making smart choices when spending significant amounts of money is crucial for maintaining financial health and ensuring that you get the best value for your investment. By conducting thorough research, considering the total cost of ownership, timing your purchase wisely, and planning your finances accordingly, you can make well-informed decisions that align with your financial goals and needs. Remember, a big purchase should not only bring immediate satisfaction but also fit into your long-term financial plan without undue strain.

Learning from big purchase experiences

Significant purchases not only impact our immediate financial situation but also offer valuable learning opportunities. Reflecting on these experiences, whether they resulted in success or revealed mistakes, can provide profound insights into personal financial habits, decision-making processes, and planning skills. This expanded section explores how to extract and apply lessons from big purchase experiences for future financial growth and wisdom.

1. **Reflecting on the Decision-Making Process**
    - **Evaluating the Research Phase**: Look back at how you researched and prepared for the purchase. Were there areas where more thorough research could have provided better insights?

    - **Assessing the Needs vs. Wants Analysis**: Reflect on how effectively you differentiated between needs and wants. Consider whether the purchase fulfilled a genuine need or if it was more influenced by desire or external pressures.

2. Reviewing Financial Planning and Budgeting

- **Budget Impact Analysis**: Assess how the purchase impacted your overall budget and financial goals. Did it lead to financial strain, or were you well-prepared for it?

- **Savings Strategy Review**: Evaluate the effectiveness of your saving strategy. Was it sufficient, or could different saving approaches have been more beneficial?

3. Lessons from Financing and Payment Choices

- **Financing Decisions**: If you financed the purchase, reflect on the terms and conditions of the financing. Were they favorable, or did they add unnecessary financial burden?

- **Payment Method Analysis**: Consider whether the payment method chosen was the most efficient. For example, could paying upfront have saved more money in the long term compared to financing or vice versa?

4. Understanding the Emotional Aspects

- **Emotional Influences**: Recognize any emotional influences that impacted your purchase decision. Did emotions like excitement or peer pressure play a role, and how might this awareness guide future decisions?

- **Buyer's Remorse or Satisfaction**: Reflect on your feelings post-purchase. If there's buyer's remorse, what contributed to it? If there's satisfaction, what factors led to this positive outcome?

5. Learning from Successes and Mistakes

- **Analyzing Successful Outcomes**: Identify what went well and why. Understanding the factors that contributed to a successful purchase can help replicate these strategies in the future.

- **Learning from Mistakes**: If the purchase didn't turn out as expected, identify what went wrong. Was it a lack of research, poor timing, or not sticking to the budget? Use these insights to make more informed decisions in the future.

6. **Sharing and Discussing with Others**
   - **Engaging in Financial Conversations**: Share your experiences with family, friends, or financial advisors. Discussions can provide additional perspectives and advice.
   - **Mentoring Others**: Use your experience to mentor others who might be facing similar purchasing decisions. Sharing your insights can help them navigate their financial journeys.

7. **Documenting and Reviewing**
   - **Keeping a Financial Journal**: Document these big purchase experiences in a financial journal. This can be a valuable resource for future reference.
   - **Periodic Reviews**: Periodically review past big purchases and the lessons learned. This ongoing process can continually refine your financial acumen.

Every significant purchase offers a chance to learn and grow financially. By reflecting on these experiences, assessing both the successes and shortcomings, and openly discussing and sharing these lessons, individuals can build a more robust, informed, and effective approach to managing their finances. These lessons become invaluable tools for navigating future financial decisions, enhancing one's ability to achieve financial goals and stability.

6.3 Future Financial Planning

Planning for the future is a critical aspect of financial management. It involves not only preparing for short-term goals and upcoming expenditures but also looking ahead to long-term objectives and eventualities. This section will cover simple but effective strategies for future financial planning, the basics of estate planning and wills, and the importance of discussing and setting long-term financial goals.

Simple Ways to Plan for the Future

Planning for the future financially is about setting a roadmap for your life's goals and unexpected events. Here's an in-depth look at simple yet effective strategies for future planning:

1. **Goal Setting**: Begin with clear, specific, and achievable financial goals. These could range from buying a home, saving for retirement, to funding education. Break these into short-term, medium-term, and long-term goals.

2. **Budgeting for the Future**: Develop a budget that includes savings for future

goals. Allocate a portion of your income regularly to different goals, adjusting as your financial situation changes.

3. **Building an Emergency Fund**: Create an emergency fund to cover unexpected life events like job loss or medical emergencies. A good rule of thumb is to have three to six months' worth of living expenses saved.

4. **Investing Wisely**: Look into different investment options like stocks, bonds, mutual funds, or real estate for long-term growth. Consider talking to a financial advisor to choose the right investment mix based on your risk tolerance and time horizon.

5. **Regular Review and Adjustment**: Periodically review your financial plan to adjust for life changes like a new job, marriage, or the birth of a child. Flexibility in your plan is key to adapting to life's uncertainties.

Basic Estate Planning and Wills

Estate planning is about ensuring your assets are managed and distributed according to your wishes after your death. Here's how to approach it:

1. **Creating a Will**: A will is a legal document that details how you want your assets distributed. Without a will, the state decides how to distribute your assets, which might not align with your wishes.

2. **Consider a Living Trust**: A living trust can help manage your assets while you're alive and distribute them after your death, often bypassing the lengthy and public probate process.

3. **Healthcare Directives and Power of Attorney**: Assign a healthcare power of attorney to make medical decisions if you're unable and create a living will to outline your wishes for medical care.

4. **Designating Beneficiaries**: Ensure all your accounts, especially retirement accounts and life insurance policies, have designated beneficiaries.

5. **Seek Professional Help**: Estate planning can be complex, involving various legal and tax implications. Consulting with an estate planning attorney or financial advisor is advisable.

Discussing Long-Term Financial Goals

Long-term financial goals require forward-thinking and ongoing conversations. Here's how to approach these discussions:

1. **Open Family Discussions**: Regularly discuss long-term financial goals with family members. Whether it's planning for retirement, buying a house, or saving for children's education, ensure everyone understands and supports these goals.

2. **Retirement Planning**: Discuss when and how you plan to retire, including the lifestyle you wish to maintain and how you're preparing financially.

3. **Education Goals**: If you have children, plan for their education early. Discuss saving strategies like education savings accounts or college funds.

4. **Big Life Events**: Plan for major life events like buying a home or starting a business. Discuss the financial implications and necessary steps to achieve these goals.

5. **Legacy Planning**: Talk about how you wish to leave your assets to family members or charities and the impact you hope to make.

Comprehensive financial planning involves preparing for your immediate needs while keeping an eye on the future. By setting and discussing clear goals, engaging in estate planning, and creating a flexible financial plan, you can ensure that you're prepared for what life brings. Regular reviews and adjustments to your plans help keep your financial journey on track.

6.4 Life Changes and Money

Financial Planning for Life Events (Marriage, Home)

Financial planning for significant life events like marriage and buying a home requires foresight, adaptability, and a clear understanding of your financial landscape.

When planning for marriage, it's crucial to have open conversations with your partner about your financial beliefs, debts, and goals. This transparency lays the groundwork for a shared financial strategy. Couples should consider creating a joint budget, which accounts for combined income and expenses, and plan for short-term and long-term goals, like vacations or retirement. It's also wise to discuss how to manage existing debts and whether to merge bank accounts or maintain individual ones.

Buying a home, another pivotal life event, demands thorough financial preparation. This process typically begins with saving for a down payment, which can be facilitated by setting aside a portion of your monthly income into a dedicated savings account. A clear understanding of your credit score and how it impacts mortgage options is crucial. Additionally, it's important to budget for other home-buying costs, such as closing fees, home inspections, and potential renovations. Prospective homeowners should also plan for ongoing expenses, like property taxes, homeowners insurance, and maintenance costs.

Both these life events – marriage and homeownership – require regular revisiting of your financial plan to align with your changing needs and circumstances.

Adjusting Financial Strategies for Life Changes

Life is dynamic, and significant changes such as a career shift, the birth of a child, or unexpected health issues necessitate adjustments in financial strategies. When life changes occur, reevaluate your budget to reflect your new income or expenses. For instance, a career change might bring a different salary, requiring adjustments to saving and spending patterns.

The addition of a family member, like the birth of a child, introduces new financial demands – from immediate needs like baby supplies to long-term considerations like education funds. It's essential to adjust your budget and savings plan to accommodate these changes.

In the case of unexpected life events, such as health issues, an emergency fund becomes indispensable. Such funds can cushion the financial impact and alleviate stress. It's also a reminder of the importance of having adequate health insurance and possibly, disability insurance, to protect against unforeseen medical expenses.

Preparing Kids for Financial Independence

Preparing kids for financial independence is a gradual process that involves educating them about money management from an early age. Start with simple concepts like saving and the value of money, gradually introducing more complex ideas as they grow older.

Encourage teenagers to take part-time jobs or summer internships. Earning their own money teaches them about the working world and the value of a dollar. It also provides practical experience in managing their own finances.

Teaching budgeting is critical. Help them create a budget for their earnings or allowances, guiding them to allocate funds for saving, spending, and giving. This practice instills the habit of not living beyond their means.

Introduce them to banking, showing them how to manage a checking and savings account. Discussions about credit, including the proper use of credit cards and understanding credit scores, are also essential.

Lastly, involve them in family financial discussions about bills, household budgeting, and saving for big-ticket items. This inclusion gives them a broader perspective on financial management and prepares them for their own financial responsibilities in adulthood.

In summary, adapting your financial strategies to accommodate life changes and preparing children for financial independence are ongoing processes that require flexibility, planning, and continuous education. Whether it's adjusting your budget after a significant life event or instilling financial literacy in your children, these steps are crucial in maintaining financial health and readiness for the future.

6.5 Ethical and Sustainable Money Choices
Teaching Kids About Ethical Spending

Educating children about ethical spending involves guiding them to make purchasing decisions that are not only good for them but also for society and the environment.

1. **Understanding Ethical Spending**: Begin by explaining what ethical spending means – choosing products and services that are produced responsibly, respecting human rights, animal welfare, and the environment.

2. **Researching Products and Companies**: Teach children how to research products and companies. Show them how to find information about a company's business practices, such as if they use fair labor practices or have environmentally friendly policies.

3. **Quality Over Quantity**: Encourage them to buy fewer but higher-quality items that last longer, rather than numerous cheaply made products. This reduces waste and often supports better production practices.

4. **Supporting Local and Ethical Businesses**: Introduce them to the concept of supporting local businesses and artisans, which not only fosters community growth but often involves more ethical practices compared to mass production.

5. **Practical Activities**: Involve them in shopping decisions. For example, when grocery shopping, discuss the benefits of buying organic or locally produced food.

Simple Ways to Make Money Choices Sustainable

Making sustainable money choices involves considering the long-term environmental and societal impact of our financial decisions.

1. **Green Banking**: Consider using banks that have environmentally friendly policies or that invest in sustainable projects. Some banks and investment funds specifically focus on environmental sustainability.

2. **Eco-friendly Products and Services**: Opt for products and services that are environmentally friendly. This might include energy-efficient appliances, sustainable clothing brands, or electric vehicles.

3. **Reducing, Reusing, Recycling**: Embrace the philosophy of reducing waste, reusing items, and recycling. This can be as simple as using reusable bags and containers, buying second-hand items, or recycling electronics.

4. **Investing in Sustainable Funds**: For long-term investments, look into funds or stocks that support sustainable businesses. Many investment options now focus on companies with strong environmental and social governance (ESG) criteria.

5. **Minimizing Resource Consumption**: Be mindful of everyday resource consumption. Saving water, reducing energy use, and minimizing carbon footprints are all part of sustainable money choices.

Discussing the Impact of Money on the Environment

The impact of money on the environment is a complex subject, encompassing how financial decisions at both the individual and corporate levels affect the planet.

1. **Consumer Impact**: Discuss how consumer choices can have a direct impact on the environment. For example, buying products with excessive packaging contributes to waste, while opting for sustainably produced items can reduce environmental harm.

2. **Corporate Responsibility**: Talk about how companies' operations can have significant environmental impacts. This includes their use of resources, handling of waste, and carbon footprint.

3. **Investment and Funding**: Explain how investments can drive environmental

outcomes. Money invested in fossil fuels, for instance, has a different environmental impact compared to investment in renewable energy.

4. **Role of Governments and Policy**: Discuss how government policies and where they allocate funds (such as subsidies for renewable energy vs. fossil fuels) can greatly impact environmental outcomes.

5. **Personal Responsibility and Advocacy**: Emphasize that individual actions and advocacy for environmentally responsible spending and investment can contribute to larger change.

Educating about ethical spending, sustainable money choices, and the financial impact on the environment is crucial in shaping responsible future consumers and investors. These lessons help children understand the broader implications of their financial actions and encourage them to contribute positively to society and the environment.

Chapter Eight

Learning about Financial Changes

Keeping Up with Simple Financial News

Staying informed about financial news is crucial for making educated financial decisions. It involves understanding market trends, economic policies, and how they affect personal finance. Here's a detailed approach:

1. **Selecting Reliable News Sources**: Begin by identifying credible and accessible financial news sources. This could include financial news websites, newspapers, and reputable blogs. Avoid sources with sensational or biased reporting.

2. **Regular Check-Ins**: Set aside a regular time each day or week to check financial news. This could be part of your morning routine or during a lunch break.

3. **Using Financial News Apps**: Utilize financial news apps that provide up-to-date market news, analysis, and insights. Many of these apps can be customized to focus on topics of personal interest.

4. **Understanding Basic Economic Indicators**: Familiarize yourself with basic economic indicators like inflation rates, unemployment rates, GDP growth, and how they affect the economy and personal finance.

5. **Financial Podcasts and Videos**: Listen to financial podcasts or watch video segments that explain current financial events in a straightforward manner. These can often provide deeper insights than written news.

6. **Community Discussion Forums**: Participate in online forums or local community groups where financial news is discussed. This can provide diverse perspectives and help clarify complex topics.

Teaching Kids to Stay Informed About Money

Educating children about money involves more than just saving and spending; it also includes understanding the financial world. Here's how to guide them:

1. **Simple Financial Discussions**: Start with basic discussions about money. Explain how the economy works in simple terms - like how prices are determined, what taxes are for, and why people invest.

2. **Kid-Friendly Financial News Resources**: Introduce them to child-friendly financial news resources. There are websites, apps, and publications designed to explain financial concepts and news to children.

3. **Incorporate News into Daily Conversations**: Regularly talk about financial news at home. Discuss things like changes in prices (inflation), new technological advancements (like electric cars), or big economic events in terms that they can understand.

4. **Practical Money-Related Activities**: Engage them in activities that involve money decisions, like grocery shopping on a budget, planning a family outing with a set amount of money, or a simple project to earn extra pocket money.

Fun Ways to Learn About Economic Changes

Learning about economics and financial changes can be engaging and enjoyable. Here are some fun ways to incorporate this learning:

1. **Economic Board Games**: Play board games that involve economic concepts. Games like Monopoly, The Game of Life, or Catan can teach principles of economics, trading, and financial planning.

2. **Interactive Online Tools and Games**: Use interactive online tools and games designed to teach economic concepts. These can range from simple budgeting games to more complex simulations of market trends.

3. **Role-Playing Activities**: Create role-playing scenarios where kids have to make financial decisions, like running a mock business or managing a household

budget.

4. **Field Trips**: Organize visits to local businesses or financial institutions. Many banks and companies offer educational programs for students to learn about economics and finance.

5. **Financial Documentaries and Shows**: Watch age-appropriate documentaries or TV shows that focus on economics and finance. Discuss the content afterward to reinforce learning.

Educating about financial news and economics doesn't have to be daunting. By keeping it simple, relevant, and interactive, you can spark an interest in financial matters that will serve children well into adulthood. These approaches provide the foundational knowledge necessary to navigate the financial world confidently.

7.2 Embracing Financial Technology
Simple Introduction to FinTech
Understanding FinTech in Today's World

FinTech, or financial technology, refers to the integration of technology into offerings by financial services companies to improve their use and delivery to consumers. Here's a comprehensive introduction:

1. **Defining FinTech**: Explain FinTech as the application of technology to improve financial activities. It encompasses a broad range of products, services, and businesses that use software and modern technology to provide financial services.

2. **Examples of FinTech**: Introduce common examples of FinTech, such as mobile banking apps, online investment platforms, digital wallets like PayPal or Venmo, robo-advisors for investing, and cryptocurrencies like Bitcoin.

3. **Benefits of FinTech**: Discuss how FinTech offers convenience (banking from a smartphone), efficiency (faster transactions), accessibility (banking services for those without access to traditional banks), and personalization (customized financial advice).

4. **The Evolution of FinTech**: Highlight how FinTech has evolved from ATMs and credit cards to sophisticated software and apps. Emphasize its role in democratizing financial services.

Safe Ways to Use Financial Technology
Ensuring Security and Privacy in the Digital Financial World
With the rise of FinTech, it's crucial to use these technologies safely. Here's how:

1. **Secure Internet Connections**: Always use a secure internet connection when using financial apps or platforms. Public Wi-Fi can be vulnerable to hacking.

2. **Strong Passwords and Authentication**: Use strong, unique passwords for each financial account. Enable two-factor authentication for added security.

3. **Regular Monitoring of Accounts**: Frequently check your financial accounts for unauthorized transactions. Quick detection of unusual activity can prevent significant losses.

4. **Staying Informed about Scams**: Educate yourself and your family about common online financial scams and phishing attacks. Be cautious about sharing financial information online.

5. **Using Reputable Apps and Services**: Only use financial apps and services from reputable companies. Check reviews and research the company before providing any personal or financial information.

6. **Software and App Updates**: Regularly update your financial apps and your device's operating system to ensure you have the latest security features.

Preparing for the Digital Money Future
Adapting to the Evolving Landscape of Digital Finance
The future of money is increasingly digital. Preparing for this future involves understanding and adapting to new financial technologies.

1. **Educational Resources**: Utilize online resources, courses, and webinars to stay informed about emerging FinTech trends, digital currencies, and new payment technologies.

2. **Experimenting with Digital Wallets**: Start using digital wallets and contactless payments for small transactions to become comfortable with these technologies.

3. **Understanding Digital Currencies**: Learn about digital currencies and

blockchain technology. While not necessary to invest in them, understanding their impact on the financial world is beneficial.

4. **Adopting Mobile Banking**: If you haven't already, start using mobile banking services. These platforms often offer tools for budgeting, saving, and investing.

5. **Future of Work and FinTech**: Understand how the gig economy and remote work trends are tied to FinTech solutions, such as mobile payments and freelance platforms.

6. **Involving the Family**: Discuss these changes and new technologies with your family. Encourage children and older family members to become familiar with digital financial tools, ensuring they are not left behind in the digital shift.

A basic understanding of FinTech, safe usage practices, and preparing for the digital money future are essential components of modern financial literacy. As the financial landscape evolves, staying informed and adaptable ensures that you can make the most of the opportunities and challenges presented by these advancements.

7.3 Global Money Perspectives

Basic Understanding of Global Finance

Exploring the Complexities of the World's Financial Systems

Global finance encompasses the financial systems and economic activities that connect countries around the world. It's a vast field, but here's a comprehensive introduction:

1. **Overview of Global Finance**: Explain global finance as the study of how countries manage their financial activities, including borrowing, lending, investment, trade, and currency exchange. It involves understanding how different countries' economies interact and affect each other.

2. **The Role of Major Financial Institutions**: Introduce institutions like the International Monetary Fund (IMF), World Bank, and World Trade Organization (WTO). Explain their roles in regulating and supporting international financial activities, like stabilizing economies and fostering global trade.

3. **Understanding International Trade**: Discuss how countries trade goods and services with each other, and the importance of balance of trade. Explain concepts like trade deficits and surpluses.

4. **Impact of Global Events**: Highlight how global events, like political changes, pandemics, or economic crises, can impact global finance. Discuss recent examples such as the financial implications of the COVID-19 pandemic.

5. **Currency Exchange and Foreign Exchange Markets**: Explain how currency exchange works and its importance in global trade. Discuss foreign exchange markets where currencies are traded.

Discussing Different Currencies and Economies
Navigating the World of Diverse Financial Systems

Understanding different currencies and economies is key to grasping global finance:

1. **Major World Currencies**: Introduce major world currencies like the US Dollar, Euro, British Pound, Japanese Yen, and Chinese Yuan. Discuss their roles in global trade and finance.

2. **Economic Systems**: Explain different types of economic systems (capitalist, socialist, mixed economies) and how they influence a country's financial decisions and policies.

3. **Economic Indicators**: Teach about key economic indicators used to assess a country's economic health, such as GDP, inflation rate, unemployment rate, and consumer spending.

4. **Currency Valuation and Exchange Rates**: Discuss how and why the value of a currency can change and what exchange rates mean. Explain factors that influence currency values like interest rates, economic stability, and trade relations.

Fun Global Finance Activities for Kids
Engaging and Educational Financial Exercises for Young Minds

Teaching kids about global finance can be fun and interactive:

1. **Currency Collection**: Start a currency collection, gathering coins and banknotes from different countries. Use this collection to discuss the countries, their economies, and cultures.

2. **Mock Stock Market Game**: Create a mock stock market game where kids can 'invest' in companies from around the world. This introduces them to the stock market and the concept of investment risk and return.

3. **Global Finance Quiz Nights**: Host quiz nights with questions about global finance, different currencies, and world economies. Make it fun with rewards for correct answers.

4. **Interactive Online Games**: Utilize online games and apps that simulate global financial activities, like running a business with international trade.

5. **World Economy Map**: Create a map highlighting different countries and their key economic indicators. Use this as a visual tool to discuss global economic disparities.

6. **Family Discussions on World News**: Regularly discuss international news stories related to finance and economy. Relate these stories to the concepts they have learned.

In summary, understanding global finance, currencies, and economies requires an exploration of how financial systems are interconnected globally. Teaching these concepts to kids can be made enjoyable through practical activities and interactive learning. This foundational knowledge is crucial in today's increasingly interconnected world and prepares them to better understand complex financial dynamics.

7.4 Continuous Financial Learning
Encouraging Lifelong Financial Education
Fostering Continuous Financial Learning and Growth

Lifelong financial education is crucial for navigating the ever-evolving financial landscape effectively. Here's how to encourage and maintain continuous learning:

1. **Embracing a Growth Mindset**: Cultivate a mindset that views financial education as an ongoing journey. Encourage the belief that there is always something new to learn, regardless of age or financial status.

2. **Staying Informed About Financial Trends**: Keep up with the latest financial trends and changes, such as new investment strategies, changes in tax laws, or emerging technologies like blockchain and digital currencies.

3. **Regular Financial Health Check-Ups**: Just as one might have regular health check-ups, schedule periodic reviews of your financial health. This includes reassessing your budget, investments, retirement plans, and insurance coverage.

4. **Attending Workshops and Seminars**: Participate in financial workshops and seminars. Many banks, community centers, and online platforms offer sessions on various financial topics.

5. **Utilizing Online Courses and Webinars**: Take advantage of online courses and webinars. Platforms like Coursera, Udemy, and Khan Academy offer courses in personal finance, investment, economics, and more.

Simple Resources for Ongoing Learning
Utilizing Accessible Tools for Continuous Financial Education

There are numerous resources available for those looking to expand their financial knowledge. Here's a selection of simple and accessible tools:

1. **Financial News Websites and Blogs**: Regularly visit financial news websites and follow finance blogs for up-to-date information and insightful analysis.

2. **Podcasts and YouTube Channels**: Listen to financial podcasts and follow YouTube channels dedicated to finance. These can provide valuable insights in an easily digestible format.

3. **Personal Finance Books**: Build a library of personal finance books that cover a range of topics from budgeting and saving to investing and retirement planning.

4. **Financial Planning Software and Apps**: Use financial planning software and apps to manage your budget, track investments, and analyze spending patterns.

5. **Community College Courses**: Local community colleges often offer affordable courses in accounting, personal finance, and investing.

Making Financial Learning a Family Activity
Integrating Financial Education into Family Life

Incorporating financial learning into family activities can be both fun and educational. Here are some ways to make financial education a part of family life:

1. **Family Budget Meetings**: Hold regular family meetings to discuss the household budget, upcoming expenses, and financial goals. This is a great way to teach children about budgeting and planning.

2. **Investment Clubs**: Start a family investment club where each member con-

tributes ideas on stocks, bonds, or other investments. Discuss different investment options and what makes them sound or risky.

3. **Financial Board Games**: Play board games that involve financial decision-making, like Monopoly or Cashflow. These games can make learning about finance fun and interactive.

4. **Charitable Giving Decisions**: Involve the whole family in decisions about charitable giving. This teaches children about philanthropy and the impact of financial decisions on others.

5. **Grocery Shopping on a Budget**: Turn grocery shopping into a learning experience by setting a budget and involving kids in purchasing decisions. This can teach them about price comparison and budgeting.

Encouraging lifelong financial education, utilizing simple learning resources, and making financial learning a family activity are essential steps in building financial literacy and responsibility. By continuously seeking knowledge and integrating financial discussions into everyday life, individuals and families can better prepare for financial challenges and opportunities.

7.5 Adapting to Economic Shifts
Preparing for Financial Ups and Downs
Strategies for Navigating Economic Fluctuations

Financial stability often involves navigating through various ups and downs. Here's a comprehensive approach to preparing for these inevitable fluctuations:

1. **Building a Robust Emergency Fund**: One of the fundamental steps in preparing for financial uncertainties is establishing a solid emergency fund. Aim to save enough to cover at least 3-6 months of living expenses.

2. **Diversifying Income Sources**: Reduce the risk of financial instability by diversifying income sources. This could mean having multiple streams of income, such as a side job, freelance work, or passive income investments.

3. **Flexible Budgeting**: Maintain a flexible budget that can be adjusted according to changes in income or expenses. This means having categories in your budget that can be scaled back when necessary.

4. **Regular Financial Reviews**: Conduct regular reviews of your financial plan to account for any changes in your financial situation, like a change in job status, income level, or family circumstances.

5. **Staying Informed**: Keep informed about economic trends and potential market changes. Understanding the economic environment can help in making proactive adjustments to your financial plan.

Simple Strategies to Handle Economic Changes
Adapting to the Evolving Economic Landscape

Economic changes can impact personal finances in significant ways. Here's how to handle these shifts effectively:

1. **Monitoring Economic Indicators**: Keep an eye on key economic indicators like inflation rates, interest rates, and employment figures. These can provide clues about the overall economic health and help you make informed financial decisions.

2. **Adjusting Investments**: Be prepared to adjust your investment strategies in response to economic changes. This might involve rebalancing your portfolio or changing your investment focus.

3. **Debt Management**: In times of economic uncertainty, prioritize managing and reducing debt, especially high-interest debt. This reduces financial vulnerability.

4. **Leveraging Economic Benefits**: Take advantage of any economic benefits or relief programs offered by governments during downturns, such as tax breaks or stimulus checks.

5. **Learning from Past Economic Cycles**: Study past economic cycles to understand how they have affected personal finances and what strategies worked best in managing them.

Teaching Flexibility and Adaptability in Finances
Cultivating a Responsive Approach to Personal Finance

Teaching financial flexibility and adaptability is crucial in preparing for an unpredictable economic future:

1. **Emphasizing the Importance of Adaptability**: Educate about the impor-

tance of being financially flexible. Discuss how economic conditions can change rapidly and the need to adjust financial plans accordingly.

2. **Scenario Planning**: Engage in scenario planning with your family. Discuss different financial scenarios, like a job loss or economic recession, and how you would respond to these situations.

3. **Encouraging Continuous Learning**: Foster a habit of continuous learning about personal finance. This could involve reading financial books, attending workshops, or engaging with financial content online.

4. **Instilling Resilience**: Teach the value of financial resilience. Share stories of how families or businesses have successfully navigated financial challenges.

5. **Modeling Flexible Financial Behavior**: Lead by example. Show how you adapt your own financial strategies in response to changing circumstances. This could involve altering spending habits, adjusting savings goals, or seeking new income opportunities.

Preparing for financial ups and downs, employing strategies to handle economic changes, and teaching flexibility and adaptability in personal finance are key to maintaining financial stability through life's many variations. These practices equip individuals and families to face economic challenges with confidence and resilience.

Chapter Nine

Conclusion

Raising Financially Smart Kids

In the essential task of raising financially smart kids, the approach is multifaceted, starting from instilling basic financial understanding to gradually introducing them to complex economic concepts. This process is not just about imparting knowledge; it's about shaping attitudes and behaviors that lead to financial prudence and responsibility.

From an early age, children can learn the basic functions of money - earning, saving, spending, and giving. These concepts can be introduced through everyday activities like grocery shopping or saving for a special toy. For instance, when children receive money as gifts or allowances, it's an opportunity to teach them about saving a portion of it, thus introducing them to the concept of delayed gratification and financial planning.

As they grow, the complexity of the financial lessons should increase. Introducing them to budgeting, for example, teaches them how to manage their resources. A practical approach could be involving them in planning a family outing or a small project, where they learn to allocate a budget effectively.

Opening a savings account for them not only introduces them to the banking system but also educates them about interest and the benefits of saving over time. This experience can be a stepping stone to more complex concepts like investments, where children can learn about stocks, bonds, and mutual funds in simple, understandable terms.

A crucial part of financial education is also understanding credit and loans. Discussions about credit cards, the importance of paying bills on time, and the consequences of debt offer vital lessons on fiscal responsibility. Explaining these concepts in relatable scenarios can make the lessons more impactful.

Furthermore, teenagers, especially, can be encouraged to take part-time jobs. This firsthand experience with earning and managing money is invaluable. It not only teaches them about the value of hard work but also about managing their own finances, making independent spending choices, and saving for their future needs.

Lastly, as part of a broader financial education, it's important to discuss risk management and the role of insurance. Children should understand the different types of financial risks and how insurance can serve as a safety net in various life situations.

Summarizing Key Financial Lessons

The journey to raise financially smart kids is built upon crucial lessons that shape their understanding and relationship with money. It starts with instilling the basics of saving and budgeting, teaching them the difference between needs and wants, and the importance of planning for future expenditures. Kids learn not only to value money but also to understand its limitations, appreciating that while it's a tool for security and comfort, true happiness often stems from non-materialistic sources.

The Journey of Financial Education

Financial education for children is a continuous process, evolving as they grow. Early lessons in simple savings accounts and understanding the concept of interest pave the way for more complex topics like investments, credit management, and ethical spending. As children mature, they are introduced to the dynamics of global finance, the impact of economic changes, and the importance of adaptability in financial planning. This education is not just about imparting knowledge but also about developing critical thinking and decision-making skills.

Inspiring a Future of Financial Confidence and Success

The ultimate goal of this financial journey is to inspire a future of financial confidence and success. By embedding financial literacy into their upbringing, children are better equipped to make informed decisions, avoid common financial pitfalls, and capitalize on opportunities to grow their wealth responsibly. They learn to navigate financial ups and downs with resilience, understanding the importance of continual learning and adaptability in an ever-changing economic landscape.

Preparing kids for financial independence, involving them in family financial discussions, and making financial education a fun and engaging part of their lives are crucial steps in this journey. This comprehensive approach ensures that children grow up to be not just financially savvy but also ethically conscious about how their financial choices impact the world around them.

In conclusion, the path to raising financially smart kids is layered and multifaceted, encompassing a wide range of topics from basic savings to global economic trends. It requires consistent effort, practical experiences, and an environment that encourages open discussions about money. With this foundation, children are well on their way to a future marked by financial confidence and success.

www.ingramcontent.com/pod-product-compliance
Lightning Source LLC
LaVergne TN
LVHW051952060526
838201LV00059B/3604